The ABC of Indoor Plants

The ABC of Indoor Plants

Jocelyn Baines and Katherine Key

Alfred A. Knopf   New York 1973

For Camilla and Ivan

This is a Borzoi Book
Published by Alfred A. Knopf, Inc.

Copyright © 1973
by Jocelyn Baines and Katherine Key

All rights reserved under International and Pan-
American Copyright Conventions. Published in
the United States by Alfred A. Knopf, Inc.,
New York. Distributed by Random House, Inc.,
New York. Originally published in Great Britain
by Michael Joseph Ltd., London

Library of Congress Cataloging in Publication Data

Baines, Jocelyn.
   The ABC of indoor plants.

   1. House plants—Dictionaries.   I. Key, Katherine,
joint author. II. Title.
SB419.B12   635.9′65′03   73-4252
ISBN 0-394-48774-5

Manufactured in Great Britain
First American Edition 1973
Second printing 1974

Contents

Introduction

Once the rockets go up,
who cares where they come down?
'That's not my department,'
says Werner von Braun

– Tom Lehrer

Such is apt, not unnaturally, to be the attitude of many, though not all, of those commercially concerned with the purveying of house plants. Their prime object is to tempt the potential customer with the most splendid display of flowers or foliage that they can produce. What happens afterwards is, provided that the plant has not been over-forced, justifiably regarded as the customer's responsibility.* All too often, a magnificently healthy plant will give its owner great satisfaction for a month or so, admittedly good value when compared with cut flowers, then begin to wilt and finally come to a wretched, neglected end: worse still it may not even survive the transfer from a shop or nursery to a house and may start to shed leaves and buds immediately.

It is the aim of this book both to help broaden the horizon of those who dare not look beyond a tradescantia, *Ficus elastica* (Indiarubber Plant) or a philodendron and at the same time to enable them to get the maximum pleasure from their plants for the longest possible time.

The principles that form the basis of success with house plants are quite easy to grasp. It is more difficult to put them into practice successfully. This is because almost all the most interesting house plants grow naturally in the rainy tropics. Thus the conditions in which they thrive are the precise opposite of those that prevail in the normal household in a temperate climate. That is to say that these plants like a high temperature, a high degree of humidity and, in the majority of cases, of flowering plants at least, strong light for some of the day. Houses, on the other hand, are all too likely to have a dry, hot atmosphere which is harmful to many plants, a cold damp one which they dislike, or one that alternates day and night between the two, which is lethal; and, particularly in towns, the area assigned to the plants such as the drawing-room or dining-room, is apt to be deficient in light.

The task then is to try, with the help of various aids, to adjust the conditions immediately surrounding the plants to simulate as closely as possible those of their natural habitat.

'It's not the humidity; it's the heat.' – Old American saying.

Temperature
Most house plants like a temperature between 25° (77°F) by day and 10° (50°F) by night during their active season, which is usually in the summer,* and do not need a temperature above 15° (59°F) during the day when they are comparatively inactive. Although most plants with which this book is concerned can stand a temperature at night as low as 5° (41°F), it is unwise to let it fall below 10°. If you are keeping your plants in a special place outside the range of the normal heating system, or if you have no central heating at night, a paraffin stove is the cheapest and the most satisfactory supplement.

Moisture
Temperature as such does not usually cause much difficulty. The great, in fact the greatest, problem is the maintenance of a moist atmosphere in conjunction with warmth.

Watering. A plant's primary food and water intake is usually through its roots and the way in which the roots are kept moist is therefore crucial: both under- and over-watering, at their extremes, can be lethal, because the process of absorbing nutrient is interfered with or, in extreme cases, arrested. It must be remembered that except in special circumstances (such as when bulbs are being dried off for storage) the soil around the roots must never be allowed to dry out completely. It must be kept constantly slightly moist – not just an inch or so below the surface but right down to the bottom of the pot (where most of the roots will usually be). Equally important – apart from bog or water plants – the soil must *only* be moist; it must not be wet. Experience alone, which is not difficult to acquire, will enable anyone to become an expert judge of the moisture required.

The hazards of under- and over-watering are most easily avoided by standing the pot or pots in a larger bowl or tray on a surface of porous pebbles,** of peat and sand mixed with crocks or pebbles, or in a special plant dish with raised ribs on the surface,*** and watering from the bottom. In this way, as long as the soil at the top of the pot is moist and there is moisture at the base, you can be sure that it is moist throughout. On no account – again except in the case of bog and water plants – allow water to stand more than fractionally above the bottom of the pot for any length of time or you will risk damaging the plant irreparably. That is why a firm porous base or a partially raised surface beneath the pot is so important. If you just have peat or a mixture of peat and sand it is easy for this to become waterlogged without your realising it and damage will be done.

If, on the other hand, you water from the top, which is conventionally the easiest way, you should first ensure that the soil is fully embedded in the pot; if it has dried out too much there will be a gap between the soil and the surface of the pot down which the water will trickle without permeating the soil. You should also see that there is a big enough space –

---

* There are now, at last, some indications that this attitude is changing: several growers provide short 'Cultivation Notes' with the plants, and vendors are more forthcoming.

* We have found that a number of Southern Hemisphere plants that would in natural conditions flower in the Northern Hemisphere winter adapt themselves to their new conditions and flower in the Northern summer. The surest winter flowerers are those from the high temperature regions of *Northern* hemisphere tropics or sub-tropics.

** In the U.K. available commercially as Substral Stenetter.

*** There are some of excellent design manufactured by Bülach Vetropack A.G. of Switzerland.

from half to one and a half inches depending on the size of the pot – between the surface of the soil and the rim of the pot, otherwise the water will simply overflow and make watering a long and messy job. Finally – and this is the crucial point – you should have a drainage system that allows you to see the water seep out of the bottom of the pot. Immediately this happens, stop watering, and if the water shows signs of remaining in the dish above the bottom of the pot remove the pot temporarily or tip the excess water away.

In certain cases, particularly where you may be keeping plants in small pots as with *Saintpaulia* (African Violets) and the danger of the soil becoming too dry is increased, it may be advisable to pack damp peat in a larger container up to the rim of the pot. The danger of over-watering will then of course be increased and it is essential to ensure that water does not accumulate in the outer container above the bottom of the flower pot. Undoubtedly the safest method for dealing with a plant that needs a high degree of moisture when you have it in a small pot is to pack the pot with peat and crocks in a larger pot or container *that itself has drainage* (i.e. holes in the bottom) and treat the whole container in the way that we have advised for larger pots. Of course this bottom container should not be put directly on a polished wood surface or one that moisture might damage. It may be stood on a tile or suchlike but not on a cork or rush mat which will merely go mouldy and aggravate any damage.

Other guidelines on watering are little more than common sense. For instance, the hotter and drier the atmosphere the more often the plants will need watering. Small pots dry out more quickly than large ones and so on. Finally, water must always be given at room temperature. Rainwater is preferable but not readily available to most people; if it is used it must have been stood indoors or otherwise have had the chill taken off. Tap water should be just warm to the touch.

Humidity. Alas, however, even with perfect watering plants may still show acute signs of distress because the atmosphere surrounding them may lack enough humidity. Only very few categories of house plants, such as most cacti, thrive in a hot, dry atmosphere. Most others will quickly lose their foliage and their buds or in other ways show that all is not well. One must try to counter-balance the dry heat generated by electricity, gas, coal or central heating with a degree of moisture that will maintain the relative humidity at, ideally, 55% to 65% of the room temperature.* Most plants will be happy with 50% but in general the higher the degree of humidity that you can maintain with a high temperature the better results you will get.

Unless you keep your plants in a special room or in a conservatory, primitive devices for the raising of humidity such as bowls or pans of water in front of the heat generators are not very effective. You have to concentrate on the area immediately round the plant or plants. Here, an expanse of water certainly does help and it is possible without much ingenuity to have an ornamental bowl of water, with perhaps some water plants in it, at the centre of a group of house plants, or some far more ambitious and elaborate pool in a conservatory. Then, a bed of Stenetter pebbles or of moist peat, sand and crocks, as suggested, in a tray or bowl on which the pot is placed, will help appreciably. Further, plants will benefit greatly from frequent syringing of their leaves; some, such as gardenias, rely on their foliage as an important means of absorbing extra moisture, while for the bromeliads and other epiphytic plants the atmosphere is the only or the most important source of all nutrition. The syringing must be done with water at room temperature and it is infinitely preferable that it should be rain water than tap water whose high lime content may leave unsightly white markings on the leaves. But rainwater is not always easy to come by and in the case of foliage plants, at least, it is worth using distilled water or water from a defrosted refrigerator. There are now some very effective fine mist sprays on the market.

Unfortunately, none of these remedies has much effect if the atmosphere is very dry. The best, in fact the only wholly satisfactory, course for the serious indoor plant grower is to invest in some humidifiers, either simple ones that are hung on radiators (if this applies) or the more elaborate and much more effective electrically powered ones. Even if this course is not followed, it is at least wise to have a humidity gauge where the majority of (or any especially valued) plants are kept so that short-term remedial action can be taken in time if it becomes necessary.

The importance of the right amount of humidity cannot be over-emphasised, particularly when plants have just been bought or brought in from a greenhouse or conservatory. More disappointments are caused by a sudden, prolonged 20% drop in humidity than by any other factor. But plants are fairly adaptable provided that they are given enough time. It is essential to make no sudden, drastic change in their way of life. Thus the conditions in which the plants have lived for a period before being brought into the house should be carefully checked and simulated as closely as possible at first (even if those conditions were not ideal); thereafter gradual adjustments can be made.

Light
After the right amount of heat and moisture, plenty of light is the third essential. Elbert and Hyams have written fully and instructively on light for house plants, including the use of artificial light and growth lamps.* We shall not deal with the matter here in so much detail and refer the reader in search of more knowledge to their book, to which we acknowledge our indebtedness.

Under natural conditions most, at least of the flowering plants, with which we are concerned receive far more light than it is possible to provide in any room, even with a glass roof. Although tropical plants will thrive on far less light than they

---

* Relative humidity is the ratio of the actual water content of the air to the maximum amount the air is capable of containing at the same temperature. Humidity gauges usually express the humidity in terms of a percentage of the temperature; e.g. if the air contained one half the water vapour needed for saturation at, say, a temperature of 20° (68°F) the relative humidity of the air would be one half and would show at 50% on the gauge. The higher the temperature, of course, the higher the saturation point.

* *House Plants*, London, 1967, pp. 32–57.

receive in nature, the light is not bright enough in many Northern countries to get anywhere near their requirements.

Elbert and Hyams estimate that five hours' direct sunlight in a day is the most that one can reasonably expect to fall on the best-placed house plant, and there are many corners, alcoves, etc. which seem to cry out for a pot plant but which get only two hours' sunlight or even none. Moreover, only that part of the plant that faces the window will get the full effect of the light because plants indoors do not benefit from the reflection and diffusion of light that occurs outside. Restricted availability of light in the house has led to growers concentrating on plants that need relatively little light. This is one major reason for the great range of foliage plants – some of which are rather dull – that are promoted. It is also one of the reasons (apart from their beauty) for the popularity of *Saintpaulia*, which Elbert and Hyams reckon to need only some two hours of sunlight in a day.

However, as so many of the most exciting plants – above all the flowering plants – need the maximum light that can be provided in a house, it is worth going to some trouble to create the best possible conditions. The first essential is to choose the lightest available position in the house as a permanent 'base' for your plants. Many plants can successfully be brought into flower in such a base and then be moved to a less well lit position to be enjoyed more fully. Once they have finished flowering they can be returned to their base. One must, however, be very careful to ensure, as has been stressed, that there is no drastic change in the temperature or humidity and that the plants are not in a draught or too close to the fumes of a gas fire or other source of artificial heat: otherwise your enjoyment will be shortlived.

The 'base' should consist of tables or suchlike, covered perhaps with oil cloth, that you do not mind getting wet from the syringing of the plants. (We have also suggested working an ornamental bowl of water into the scheme.) If you are ambitious it is worth buying one or more photographer's lamps and fitting them with 150 watt 'blue' bulbs. Such lamps are not expensive and are light and easy to manipulate. The lights should be directed onto the appropriate plants (i.e. those that are ready to be encouraged into bud, then flower) and switched on for two or more hours during daylight when they will supply some welcome additional 'blue' light from which plants benefit most.* Care should be taken to see that the light bulbs do not come too close to a plant because they generate damaging heat; also, never syringe when the light is on as the cool water may cause the bulb to explode. It is much better to give this extra light during daylight hours because many plants need the darkness at night in order to develop properly. In addition, appreciable benefit will be gained by setting up one or more light reflectors (e.g. sheets of chrome or aluminium foil) at vantage points round the 'base' so that the maximum use is made of the available light. If you are fortunate enough to have a well-placed conservatory or other area specifically devoted to plants most of the problems of light can be easily solved; otherwise, in general living rooms where the needs of the plants and aesthetic considerations clash, it is best to assess realistically how much light you can provide and concentrate on plants in the appropriate category.

The use of growth lamps and totally artificially lit gardens are specialized techniques which do not come within the scope of this book. However, this is an area of rapid innovation and increasing importance as cities become more and more built up and natural light more scarce. Some people may be excited, some dismayed by the thought that 'twelve to sixteen hours of fluorescent light daily gives plants an endless summer and an automatic timer makes this routine.'* We are used to chrysanthemums flowering all the year round; now we have marguerites and others too. Soon, due to science, flowering 'seasons' for house plants may become archaic. The use of artificial light for house plants, is still, for the majority of amateurs, unexplored territory but in the United States and elsewhere it is being imaginatively promoted and will without doubt revolutionise the world of house plants.

Nutrition and Soil

We have dealt with temperature, moisture and light. The fourth essential on which to concentrate is the plant's nutrition, obtained primarily through its roots. Here it is perhaps simplest to break down the term 'soil' into two components: the medium in which the roots of the plant are anchored – that may not be soil in the conventional sense at all – and the substances active in the 'soil' that the roots need to absorb for healthy growth.

First, the roots need water and air. The moisture requirements have already been described under *Watering*. Closely linked with watering is the aeration of the 'soil'. Plant roots take in oxygen and give out carbon dioxide which must escape through the soil to the atmosphere. Hence the need to maintain the right balance between a highly aerated, dry medium that lacks the water necessary to plant growth and a waterlogged medium that prevents all but certain categories of plant from 'breathing' adequately.** After air and water come six other elements essential to a plant's nutrition in relatively large amounts: nitrogen, phosphorus, potassium, calcium, magnesium and sulphur. In addition, various trace elements are needed, usually in minute quantities: boron, chlorine, copper, iron, manganese, molybdenum and zinc; there may be others whose usefulness has not yet been identified.

The above fulfil the plant's basic nutritional needs. And it can immediately be seen that conventional 'soil' as such need play no essential part in providing these needs; hence the efficacy of artificial 'mixes' and also of hydroponic culture.*** Natural soil does however provide a further factor that can be very beneficial (and is essential to plants not being artificially fertilised) but may also be harmful: the bacterial

---

* The best artificial light for plants is fluorescent. Terrestris of New York, in their *Indoor Plant Guide*, basing their advice on experiments conducted by the U.S. Department of Agriculture at Beltsville, Maryland, recommend cool, white fluorescent tubes. Alternatively, they suggest 'colour-improved mercury vapour bulbs'. These need expensive special fixtures but the lamps are usually more appealing aesthetically; moreover the bulbs use 60% less electricity and last ten times longer than fluorescent tubes.

* *House & Garden*, London, January 1971, p. 86.
** Water of course contains oxygen but not enough for most plants.
*** See J. Sholto Douglas, *Beginner's Guide to Hydroponics*, London and New York, 1972, for an exposition of this method by a leading authority.

activity that takes place within the soil. Bacteria feed off decaying plant roots and other matter and excrete back into the soil some of the mineral nutrient taken up by the plant roots as well as additional substances of their own: these are the brown and black substances in the soil, usually called humus. It is a natural process that improves the aeration and texture of the soil and, broadly, maintains the environmental balance. However, natural soil may also house other, harmful, organisms that feed off and infect the roots of a plant. There are various types of 'natural soils' such as sand, clay and – best of all – loam, which is a mixture of the two and has a good humus content.

Loam with additions in the form of charcoal, well-rotted manure, dried blood, etc., in proportions appropriate to the particular plant can quite well be used for pot plants. There are also available on the market artificial 'soil mixes' with or without loam (usually sterilized), scientifically prepared to meet the requirements of each of the main categories of house plant. We strongly advise the use of an appropriate 'mix', although it must be realised that certain organic processes will not take place in such a 'mix' and that there is therefore greater danger of the medium turning 'sour', above all where there is little root activity.

The John Innes and Levington composts are among the most admirable in Britain, and Black Magic soilless planting medium and Swiss Farm's potting soils in the United States. The requirements of tropical and semi-tropical plants are well met by Levington Compost or John Innes No. 2 or 3 Potting Compost. Levington Compost is very light and porous and therefore particularly good for drainage, but it requires supplemental mineral feeding more quickly than John Innes – generally after two to three months. In all cases it is important to follow carefully the manufacturer's instructions on the package.

If you do not use a proprietary compost, the following three mixtures can be made up to suit the three main categories of house plants. The first category, which we term No. 1,* is designed for tropical and sub-tropical plants. Basically, it should consist, per 6-inch pot, of:

    3 parts peat or sphagnum moss
    1 part perlite
    2 parts vermiculite
    1 part humus or leaf mould
    a heaped tablespoon each of charcoal and lime.**

The second main category of house plants comprises the cacti and some succulents. These require a soil mix that we term No. 2 and it should basically consist, per 6-inch pot, of:

    1 part garden soil (sterilized)
    1 part leaf mould or peat moss
    1 part coarse sand
    1 part small pebbles or brocken crock
    2 tablespoons bone meal
    2 teaspoons ground limestone or chips.

* Our numbering of composts should not be confused with the John Innes numbering or with that of any other commercially marketed composts.
** Lime should of course be omitted for calcifuge plants such as camellias, rhododendrons, gardenias, etc.

Swiss Farms Cactus Soil is marketed in the United States but there is as yet no manufactured mix readily available in the U.K. for this category of plant.

The third main category comprises plants of the temperate zone and requires a mix that we term No. 3. Basically it should consist, per 6-inch pot, of:

    2 parts loam or garden soil
    1 part peat moss or humus
    1 part coarse sand
    a heaped tablespoon each of dried blood and charcoal.

Orchids and bromeliads need special mixes which will be described under their entries.

The point of No. 2 mix is self-evident in as much as the soil should be quite porous when wet but should have a good 'anchoring' element because the plants concerned do not have a strong rooting system. The chief difference between No. 1 and No. 3 compost is that the latter is richer and the former is more porous with a corresponding higher degree of aeration. In fact little harm will come through planting a No. 3 category plant in a No. 1 compost provided that the plants are given liberal nourishment during their active period.

Once the basic constitution of the soil has been settled two main factors should concern the house plant grower. The first is maintaining the nutritional content and the second is ensuring the right pH balance. As we have said, commercial soil mixes often contain enough nutrient to make additional feeding superfluous for the first few months. Thereafter, during a plant's *active* season, and during that season only, an appropriate fertilizer added to water or, if in pill form, inserted in the soil, at regular intervals will have remarkably good effects. In fact such treatment is essential if you want a plant to achieve its full potential. You have only to think of the thoroughly artificial conditions in which you are expecting a plant to thrive to realise this need. Fortunately in this area at least science has enabled us to combat the constrictions of forcing a plant into a pot inside a house. There are a number of excellent fertilizers on the market and it is best to choose one that contains the trace, as well as the primary, nutritional elements. There are also effective foliar feeds commercially available which are particularly useful for rhododendrons as well as for orchids, bromeliads and other epiphytic plants. We must emphasise, in all cases, the importance of following the manufacturers' instructions very carefully. It is not only pointless, as in the human consumption of vitamins, but positively harmful (unlike, probably, the human parallel) to over-fertilize because the fertilizing agent will not just 'pass through the system' but may set up harmful side-effects, such as 'scorching' the roots or damaging the foliage.

The other important factor is to maintain the correct pH balance. The pH symbol denotes the relative acidity/alkalinity of a soil. In an arbitrary scale of numbers from 1 to 14 the lower numbers represent a high degree of acidity and the higher represent a high degree of alkalinity. Most plants demand a pH range between 4·5 and 8. The majority of house plants like a neutral, (pH7) or slightly alkaline soil; the big exceptions are rhododendrons, camellias and gardenias which demand an acid soil, of about pH5 to 6·5. There are a number of excellent marketed devices for testing the pH content of the soil. A pot plant's soil will tend to become more acid and the periodic addition of calcium nitrates, of limestone chips or eggshells is a useful corrective. In the case of acid-loving plants periodic application of potassium sulphate or iron chelate is essential.

Pots and Re-potting

We have dealt with the 'soil' but not yet with the container for the plant and the 'soil'. Here drainage is the overriding factor; thus aesthetic and practical considerations may clash. It is no use transferring a plant to a pretty container only to see it wilt and die within a couple of weeks because of deficient drainage. Fortunately, at least in our opinion, plain earthenware pots are positively pleasing, particularly after they have weathered a little, and they are as practical a means of keeping house plants as is available. In recent years plastic pots have largely displaced them in some shops, which in our view is a pity but this view is evidently not shared by many others. Practically, there is little to choose between plastic and earthenware: the former retains moisture better, so reducing the chore of watering, is lighter to carry and easier to keep clean but earthenware pots are more porous and so allow the roots of the plant to 'breathe' better. It is therefore a matter of personal choice.

Most plants will periodically become too large for their pots – or rather their roots will become too cramped. In fact plants may be bought 'pot-bound', i.e. with the roots forced into the shape of the pot. It is claimed that some plants are best kept like this because it restricts the growth of roots while encouraging a more profuse flowering. But, generally, outside the grower's expertly controlled conditions, pot-binding creates such problems in regulating the supply of water and nutrient that it is wise to give a plant a large enough pot for the roots to develop with little hindrance. But the pot must not be too large; in an area without root activity the soil is liable to turn sour.

The transfer of a plant from one pot to another of a similar size (e.g. from a plastic to an earthenware pot, or when the plant needs 'cleansing') presents no problem whatsoever and can be done at any time provided that the soil ball is neither dry nor wet – just moist. If it is dry bits of soil and root will break off and if it is too wet it will be hard to get out of the pot. It will be unnecessary to disturb the roots at all, except in the process of 'cleansing', unless they are squeezing badly out of the drainage holes; in that case the pot will have to be broken but not too violently or the sharp edges of the pieces may damage the roots. Plastic pots can be cut with strong kitchen scissors or a pair of clippers.

In the more usual case of transferring a plant to a larger pot the process is a little more delicate but again not at all difficult and can be done at any time, although it is best to do it when the plant is just at the start of its active season so that the roots are in a state to meet the challenge of new conditions and yet there is little chance of any check to growth impeding the budding or flowering process. As before, the soil ball must be just moist. The task then is to ease the roots out of the mould into which they have been forced by the shape of the pot so that they can be spread naturally in their new pot. The degree of difficulty will depend on the type of root: some roots are very easily handled without damage, others not so. Personal judgement must be used here as to how much the roots can be eased out of their mould; on one hand there should be the least possible breaking of roots but on the other the purpose of the operation will be nullified if the soil ball is allowed merely to retain its shape, because then the roots may stay that way and not penetrate the new soil at all. After re-potting, a plant should be given a thorough watering and then watered more frequently than usual until it has settled.

Disasters

Let us assume then that our house plants are well settled, in the right soil, with the right temperature, the right degree of humidity and enough light for them to thrive. Things nonetheless may still, alas, go very wrong. The main causes are likely to be:

(i) **The watering and the drainage.** We have already tried to give sound guidelines. One may nonetheless still have trouble, particularly if one has to go away for a short time leaving the care of the plants in less expert hands. Unfortunately the main symptoms of over- and under-watering can be similar: the yellowing and dropping of leaves. It must be left to personal judgement to decide which of the two has been the cause (and it should not be too difficult). The other main symptoms, which are obvious enough, are the wilting and drying of leaves in the case of under-watering and the darkening and wilting of the leaves of some plants in the case of over-watering. The remedies are simple although the damage may have gone too far (and it can happen very quickly: in a day or so) to be wholly or at least immediately repaired. When a plant has been over-watered it should be allowed to dry out completely and left in that state for several days, although the leaves should be syringed frequently. Then it should be watered with very particular care in future. When a plant has been under-watered it should be given an immediate drenching, but not left standing in water for more than half an hour, and again be watered with exceptional care until it has fully recovered. In an extreme case when a plant shows signs of dying back it should be quite drastically pruned to give a better chance of new growth forming.

(ii) **The administration of nutrient.** Again, we have given general guide-lines and have emphasised strongly the need to follow the manufacturer's instructions precisely. Over a period there will usually be an accumulation of excessive and undesirable chemical matter in the soil which may show itself in the flaking and discoloration of an earthenware pot. If you have given quite heavy nutrient throughout a season it is wise, once the dormant period has been reached, to 'cleanse' the soil by removing the plant from the pot, shaking as much soil from the roots as is possible without damaging them and re-planting it in new soil in a cleaned pot. Earthenware pots in which plants have moulded or become diseased should be thoroughly scrubbed and sterilized.

(iii) **The development of a deficiency in nutrient or the wrong pH content.** The first will be avoided if a balanced fertilizer is given; but if signs of ill health appear that do not seem to be caused by pests or disease advice should be sought, or the admirable entry on 'Nutrition, Mineral, of Garden

Plants' in the Royal Horticultural Society's *Dictionary of Gardening, Supplement* (Oxford, 2nd edition, 1969) should be consulted. We have advised on the maintenance of the correct pH value of the medium; changes in the value also have side effects in determining the behaviour of certain minerals in the soil, the most important of which in this context is that, at a pH of about 6 or above, inorganic iron becomes insoluble and plants may show signs of iron deficiency, appearing as chlorosis.* The symptoms of plants suffering from this deficiency are the yellowing of leaves and a generally unhealthy appearance. Periodic doses of sequestrene (iron chelate) will remedy this.

(iv) **Pests and predatory insects.** These are most likely to be aphis (green or black fly), white fly, mealy bug, thrips, caterpillars, scale insects and red spider mite. The illustrated chart on page 184 will help identify them but some, such as red spider mite, are so small that their presence is not usually noticeable to the naked eye until they have wrought quite a bit of damage. In fact we strongly recommend a powerful magnifying glass as part of a house plant owner's basic equipment: it will help considerably in the early recognition of something amiss. Fortunately all but the last two insects named are susceptible to the wide range of insecticides on the market. These come either in the form of an aerosol or powder to be squirted or a liquid or powder to be diluted with water, then sprayed. In most household conditions an aerosol is the most convenient form of insecticide as it does not make a mess, but it is of course less powerful or lasting than the syringing (on the upper and lower sides of the leaves) or even the total immersion of the plant, but *not* the soil, in a solution. It is as well to have both methods available. Scale insects, to which *Citrus* is particularly prone, have tough shells and are immune to many standard insecticides; they have either to be scraped individually off the bark or stems (a tedious process) or treated with a solution of nicotine sulphate or malathion. Red spider mite *ought* not to appear because it only thrives in dry conditions and the right degree of humidity in the room should prevent it. But when citrus plants, for instance, are stood outdoors in the summer they are particularly prone; patchy discoloration or yellowing of the leaves will reveal the pest's presence, usually on the underside of the leaves. A drenching with one of the solutions that claim to be effective against red spider mite, together with frequent syringing, should eliminate or, at least, control it. Slugs, earwigs and woodlice, etc., may also make their appearance and should be destroyed immediately.

As some pesticide instructions warn of probable damage only to the commoner plants we give below a table** of plants known to have been damaged by certain ingredients used in some pesticides, but it is emphasised that this is not com-

prehensive and if a plant is thought to be very delicate it is better to test the pesticide on a few leaves before enveloping the plant. It should also be emphasised that young growth is much more tender than that which is well established, and open flowers are sometimes damaged.

Asparagus – petroleum oil
Calceolaria – dimethoate
Chrysanthemum – dimethoate, ethoate-methyl, formothion. Other pesticides such as demeton-S-methyl, dichlorvos and nicotine damage some varieties and the manufacturers' lists should be consulted.
Cineraria – dimethoate, phosphamidon
Cyclamen – parathion
Ferns – malathion, azobenzene, diazinon (Maidenhair fern)
Fuchsia – petroleum oil, dimethoate
Gerbera – azobenzene, malathion
Hydrangea – BHC, dimethoate
Kalanchoe – DDT
Pilea – azobenzene, malathion
Primula – demeton-S-methyl, dimethoate
Tradescantia – dichlorvos

(v) **Actual disease, either from virus and similar infections or from mildew, fungus, root rot and suchlike.** Virus diseases are fortunately uncommon in house plants (except for orchids), as in general the only treatment is to destroy the infected plant immediately and try to prevent other plants from becoming infected by sterilizing anything that has come in contact with it. Common symptoms of virus infection are light coloured rings of dead (and therefore discoloured) cells in the leaves, and deformed growth. Rot and fungus infections of the roots can be dealt with by cutting out the infected part and treating the rest with sulphur, or an appropriate fungicidal compound. Fungus and mildew of the leaves should also be treated with fungicides and advice for particular susceptible plants will be given under their appropriate headings.

Prevention of all these disasters is, however, infinitely better than cure and is in general quite feasible (except in the case of some pests and diseases). The guide-lines already given should be scrupulously followed. Above all, plants will profit from *constant* care and attention. Without this only a few will survive and none will thrive. It is worth examining your plants every day to ensure that the general conditions are right, that the 'base' is clean, because dirt generates infection and pests, that the plants look healthy and are free from disease or pests. Virus diseases are usually transmitted by pests which doubly underlines the need to observe these precautions. Further the rooms where the plants are kept should be well ventilated; plants need fresh air and – both for their appearance as well as for their health because they 'breathe' through their foliage – the leaves should be sponged with a solution of water and milk (fifty-fifty) to remove pollution and dust whenever they seem to need it. As with all watering, the chill should be taken off the solution. Because most tap water contains lime which may make an unsightly white deposit on the leaves, the application of a proprietary leafshine preparation will help to keep them looking clean and give protection against dust. (Various leafshines are available on the market, either in

---

* Chlorosis is defined in the Royal Horticultural Society's *Dictionary of Gardening, Supplement*, Oxford, 2nd edition, 1969, as: 'Abnormal paling or yellowing of the leaves, due to destruction of or failure to form chlorophyll, the green colouring matter of plants . . . [It] may be due to many different causes including deficiency of nutrient elements, especially nitrogen, iron, or magnesium; root injury by over- or under-watering or attack by pests or diseases; unfavourable atmospheric conditions, especially too high or too low a temperature; virus disease, etc.'
** *Commercial Production of Pot Plants*, Bulletin 112, HMSO 1969, p. 103. We are indebted to this publication for the section on pests and predatory insects.

liquid form to be sponged on or – more convenient – as aerosol sprays: as usual, instructions should be read carefully beforehand as not all plants can be so treated without harm.)

To end this section on a personal note: we have found that the main causes of our own casualties have been red spider mite, detected too late, and inadvertently allowing a plant to dry out. House plants demand a lot of time and devotion and it would be silly to pretend otherwise. Given this essential attention the rewards in pleasure and interest are immense.

Propagation

Although the propagation of plants is probably outside the scope of most users of this book we have included a rudimentary guide by symbol to the methods of propagation best used for each plant, e.g. by leaf or stem cuttings, by division, by seed or by more than one of these processes.

Cuttings. There are differing opinions about the ease of taking cuttings successfully and a lot, of course, depends on the type of plant. As a very general rule the ease of cuttings varies in relation to the softness of the wood; the softer the wood the more readily, and certainly the more quickly, a cutting will take. Thus *Impatiens* (Busy Lizzie) and shrubby begonias, for instance, come at the easy end of the scale and camellias, citrus or gardenias at the difficult end.

It must also be realised that tropical plants require very special conditions for cuttings to strike and survive. They almost invariably need strong bottom heat, about 30° (86°F), and a very high humidity because the greatest danger is that of the cutting drying off. They must therefore be raised in a covered propagating tray or frame with artificial heat.* It is wise to have a thermometer inserted in the cuttings compost so as to keep a check on the temperature; those sold for tropical fish tanks do very well.

In the case of most plants the cutting should consist of a shoot of vigorous young growth about three inches long, with a short section of mature wood (the 'heel') at the base, cut cleanly. With longer shoots a nodal cutting may be more satisfactory. The node is the leaf joint and a clean cut should be made just below the node. The leaves should be gently removed from this node, as should, usually, the soft top of the shoot, and the stem dipped first in water, then up to half an inch in hormone rooting powder (easily obtainable from most gardening shops). Any bark etc. on the stem likely to collect moisture should be dusted lightly with sulphur powder because a hazard almost equal to drying out is that of the cutting going mouldy and rotting. The cutting should then be gently inserted to a depth of half an inch (or more in the case of stout shoots such as *Ficus elastica*) into a small pot of moist cuttings compost (better than standard compost) and placed on a moist base of peat or sand in the propagator, which should be shaded from direct sun. Provided that the stipulated conditions are maintained and that the cuttings are given a twice-daily ten-minute 'airing' to counteract mould the result is in the hands

* In Britain, if you have no electric propagator, the most satisfactory method is to use a Stewart propagator on top of an Aladdin greenhouse stove; a gap of about six inches must be left between the top of the stove and the propagating tray or the heat of the stove will be too intense for the cuttings (and for the tray which may melt); in fact, it is wise to put a sheet of hard asbestos between the tray and its supports.

of the gods. The gods are fickle and they frequently raise false hopes by allowing a cutting to sprout several new leaves thus encouraging one to believe that it has struck when it has not yet formed any roots and may wither immediately if removed prematurely from the propagator. It is all too easy to be premature and it must be borne in mind that many harder-wood cuttings take months rather than weeks to root.

The process of adapting a cutting that *has* struck, to life outside the propagator, is often the trickiest. It must be remembered how very intense – in terms of temperature combined with humidity – the atmosphere can be within a propagator. Thus the process of hardening off must be very, very gradual. One cannot expect a plant to experience a sudden drop of, say, 15° (27°F) in temperature and 30% to 40% in humidity and survive; therefore, after removing a rooted cutting from the propagator, every means available should be used to reduce the shock by keeping the temperature and humidity around the plant as close initially to that of the propagator as possible. The best method is perhaps to put the pot in a polythene bag, tied at the top, for several days, then gradually loosen the knot to admit air. As soon as the plant has recovered from this ordeal it should be potted on in ordinary No. 1 compost.

Many temperate zone plants do not need this intensive treatment and cuttings will strike readily without a propagator. Cuttings, such as those from camellias, that do not *need* to be enclosed should of course not be, because the hazards of propagation are thus pointlessly increased. Bottom heat is none-theless often very beneficial in this category; one camellia grower has told us that whereas he used to have an 80% failure with his cuttings he now has a 90% success over heat.

Division. Propagation by division – whether of bulbs, corms etc. or plants – speaks for itself. When a surface has actually been cut it is best as a precaution against rot to dust it with sulphur powder before re-potting the plants.

Seed. Propagation by seed, again, is relatively simple. As with cuttings, the seeds of tropical plants will almost certainly need bottom heat to germinate. It is a debatable point whether or not covering seed trays with glass or polythene sheeting is desirable, and the decision is really dictated by the degree of humidity and heat in the surrounding area. If this is high, coverings are unnecessary and will probably in fact be harmful, as they further increase heat/humidity within the tray and may cause damping off and rotting of the seeds or seedlings. If the surrounding atmosphere is on the cool and/or dry side, they are an immense help, as seedlings can dry out irreparably within hours. Either way, constant supervision of seedboxes is necessary, at least until the second or third leaf joint is reached. Glass- or polythene-covered trays must be opened out and 'aired' frequently and uncovered trays must be constantly watched to avoid drying out (watering should be done with a fine spray or through a central funnel inserted in the middle of the tray).

In general, large seeds should be sown more thinly than small ones; a common fault of the less experienced is to sow seed too closely. A made-up seed compost is best used and the seedlings should be potted on as soon as they can be dug out of the trays without damage.

Scope of this Book

The terms 'house' and 'conservatory' plants are of course artificial. We have used them to include any plant that can be grown in such an environment and that can be grown there to some purpose, in the pleasure that it will give. We have therefore excluded most plants that can equally well be grown outside in a temperate climate but have included certain categories, such as some bulbs, that can give delight indoors much earlier than they can outdoors. For a similar reason we have included plants that can be raised under glass and bedded out in the summer easily enough but which are nice to buy as house plants if you have not the facilities for raising them yourself.

For the most part, the plants listed in this book come from the rainy tropics and would not thrive outdoors much farther north or south of latitude 30°. A conservatory, a 'sun parlour' or a similar room can extend enormously the range of plants that can be grown successfully and, as we have said, it is one of our chief aims in this book to stimulate the imagination to accept the challenge of the more unusual, but sometimes quite as easy and infinitely rewarding, exotic plants.

We have therefore tried to be as comprehensive as possible within our terms of reference but ultimately of course when the category is artificial there will be an element of arbitrariness in the choice. People will wonder why such and such a plant has been chosen whereas another has been left out. Here personal taste is bound to come in. We have tried to be impartial up to a point but have not disguised our preference for plants that are 'active' rather than relatively inert, for those that flower attractively, and those that have a pleasing scent – which we look upon as one of the greatest delights that an indoor plant can give. Finally, where there is a choice, we have shown a preference on the whole for flowers that have a purity of form, for single rather than double blooms, although we have equally shown our fascination with the more exotic flower forms.

Symbols

As most of the plants described here have broadly similar requirements in care and culture there is a danger of tedious repetition of certain instructions. A series of symbols has therefore been devised, in the footsteps of the *Guide Michelin*, that summarise the main characteristics and requirements of each plant. The symbols are explained on page 15, and it is hoped that these will provide an easily grasped outline guide.

Arrangement

Each genus has a separate entry, in alphabetical order, except that certain groups of plants have for convenience been treated as a whole rather than fragmentarily; these are cacti, the more common bulbs, ferns, orchids and palms.

The families to which the genera belong are tabulated on page 186 for those wanting to specialize in any particular family.

A glossary is also provided for the more technical terms used, though we have tried to keep these to a minimum.

Acknowledgements

We are delighted to acknowledge our indebtedness to others. First, there is the Royal Horticultural Society's *Dictionary of Gardening* in four volumes (Oxford, 1965) and *Supplement* (Oxford, 1969). It is one of the most magnificent works of reference and practical application ever compiled; without it to consult we literally could not have undertaken this elementary book. It is referred to specifically in the text on relatively few occasions because it would have been tedious in such a book as this to have provided a running acknowledgement; there is however no plant entry in which we are not to some extent indebted to that great work. Then there is the American *Hortus Second* by L. H. and Ethel Zoe Bailey, a work of outstanding excellence which we have used to counter-check information. Finally, there is the magnificent *Wild Flowers of the World*, painted by Barbara Everard, text by Brian D. Morley, London and New York, 1970.

There are a number of other very valuable books on house plants, such as Rochford and Gorer's *The Rochford Book of House Plants*, London, 1961, the same authors' *The Rochford Book of Flowering Pot Plants*, London, 1966 and New York, 1964, Elbert and Hyams's *House Plants*, London, 1967 and New York, and the *Pocket Encyclopaedia of Indoor Plants in Colour*, London, 1969 and New York, 1970. Specific acknowledgements to the first three of these books are given in the text but, again, this does not take account of the wisdom and experience in the subject as a whole that all these books offer. Then another invaluable more general book is Hay and Synge's beautiful, scholarly *Dictionary of Garden Plants in Colour, with House and Greenhouse Plants*, London and New York 1969. Excellent books on specific subjects such as cacti or orchids are acknowledged in their appropriate places in the text. With the Glossary we have been guided by the R.H.S. *Dictionary of Gardening* and by A. J. Huxley's very useful *Garden Terms Simplified*, second edition, 1971.

Extract from 'Werner von Braun' taken from *Tom Lehrer's Second Song Book* by Tom Lehrer. Published by permission of Crown Publishers Inc., New York © 1968, and Elek Books Ltd., London.

We should like warmly to thank a number of nurserymen for their help; among them Thomas Butcher, Clifton Nurseries, The Flower House, P. de Jager and Sons, Hillier and Sons, Rassell's, Thomas Rochford and Sons, Thompson and Morgan, Treseders' Nurseries; the orchid specialists Burnham Nurseries, Neville Orchids, Wyld Court Orchids; and the epiphyllum and cactus specialists Auger Epiphyllums.

We are most grateful to the Director and staff of the Royal Botanic Gardens, Kew and the Director and staff of the Royal Horticultural Society's Garden at Wisley for their help in making plants available for photography; and we owe a particular debt of gratitude to Mr Ernest Crowson, F.R.P.S., A.I.I.P., for his unflagging energy and skill in photographing a large number of the plants illustrated.

Finally, we are deeply grateful to Mr Tom Wellsted for his careful reading of the text and for the many helpful suggestions that we have adopted.

Photographic Credits

We should like to thank the following copyright holders for the use of their colour transparencies:

Michael Amberger: 60.
Ernest Crowson: 31, 78, 118, 159, 179, 225, 226, 241, 254, 264.
Valerie Finnis: 19, 41, 49, 95, 113, 152, 188, 229, 267.
Anthony Huxley: 7, 112, 250, 252, 260, 261, 273.
P. de Jager & Sons: 171.
Dr George Kalmbacher: 58, 85, 86, 130, 136, 161, 174, 176, 177, 180, 187, 196.
Elsa M. Megson: 1, 80, 192, 207, 247, 253.
George Rainbird Ltd: 2, *3*, 5, 10, *13*, 15, *16*, *20*, *21*, 29, 30, 32, 33, *39*, 40, 42, 43, 44, 45, 47, 51, 53, 54, 55, 56, 62, 65, 66, 67, *68*, *71*, 72, 73, 74, 75, 76, *79*, 83, *87*, *89*, 91, 96, 99, *101*, 102, 103, *116*, *117*, 119, 121, 122, *125*, 126, 127, 128, *129*, 131, 142, *143*, 149, 153, 155, 157, 168, 172, *181*, *183*, *185*, *191*, 193, *197*, 200, 201, 202, 205, 206, 208, 212, 213, 214, 215, 218, *219*, 221, 222, 224, *238*, 242, 246, 248, 257, 263, 265, 266, 272, 275, 279, 283, 285. (Numbers in italics are reproduced by courtesy of Ilford Ltd.)
Harry Smith: 46, 52, 81, 97, 105, 106, 154, 190, 239.
G. Wells: 8, 14, 90, 132, 138, 141, 144, 184, 204, 216, 249, 277, 280.
Dennis Woodland: 194.
Our thanks are also due to Murphy Chemical Ltd., who very kindly provided the transparencies for the Pests and Diseases section, page 184.

All other photographs were specially commissioned for this book by the authors. The vast majority of these were taken by Ernest Crowson, FRPS, AIIP, to whom we have already acknowledged our great indebtedness, and other contributors were: Ellen McNeilly 12, Fred Somerset 164, 251, and Dennis Woodland 61, 93, 94, 274.

Explanation of symbols

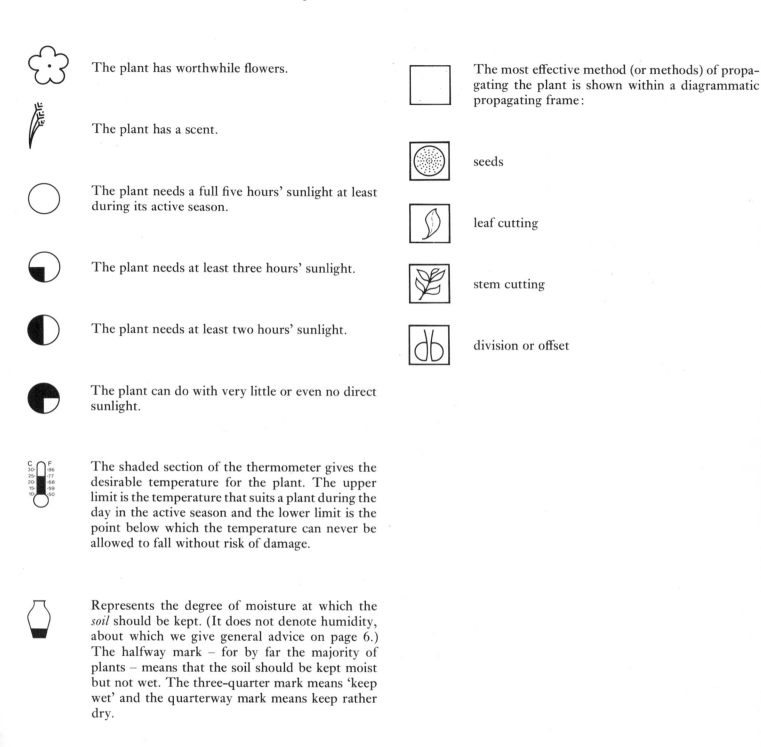

The plant has worthwhile flowers.

The plant has a scent.

The plant needs a full five hours' sunlight at least during its active season.

The plant needs at least three hours' sunlight.

The plant needs at least two hours' sunlight.

The plant can do with very little or even no direct sunlight.

The shaded section of the thermometer gives the desirable temperature for the plant. The upper limit is the temperature that suits a plant during the day in the active season and the lower limit is the point below which the temperature can never be allowed to fall without risk of damage.

Represents the degree of moisture at which the *soil* should be kept. (It does not denote humidity, about which we give general advice on page 6.) The halfway mark – for by far the majority of plants – means that the soil should be kept moist but not wet. The three-quarter mark means 'keep wet' and the quarterway mark means keep rather dry.

This indicates the soil 'mix' that is required. Explanations of Nos. 1, 2, and 3 mixes are given on page 9.

The most effective method (or methods) of propagating the plant is shown within a diagrammatic propagating frame:

seeds

leaf cutting

stem cutting

division or offset

15

Abutilon

Graceful plants with quietly pleasing, often bell-shaped, flowers, usually in combinations of yellow or white and red. Some species will grow quite tall and can be used as climbers. They have the advantage of sometimes flowering in the winter (although their habits seem to be irregular).

Abutilon bedfordianum, which will grow into a small tree, is large and handsome, with yellow petals streaked with red. *A. megapotamicum*, a shrub and perhaps the best species, has bell-shaped flowers, formed by a red calyx and yellow petals, within which the long stamens and pistils are clustered together like a bell's clapper; there is a variety with delicately

variegated leaves. *A. striatum* has orange flowers veined with red and also has a variety, *thomsonii*, with variegated leaves.

Some species, e.g. *A. megapotamicum*, will stand a temperature as low as 0° (32°F) but most are tender. They need plenty of light to bring them into flower, a temperature around 20° (68°F) and a lot of water when active, although they must never be stood in water.

Cuttings from old wood will root easily in a temperature of about 20° (68°F).

Acacia

Acacia is sold in large quantities as cut flowers in Northern countries in the winter and is seen flowering in abundance from the early spring along the Mediterranean Riviera and in similar climates. This is the 'mimosa' of florists, though the name belongs correctly to another genus (q.v.).

The delicately formed evergreen foliage and the evocative scent of the fluffy clusters of yellow pom-pom flowers make this one of the most enticing of plants to introduce into the house, although its habits provide a challenge.

There are numerous species and it is best to take what the nurseryman has to offer although checking with him whether the flowers are scented and that the tree or bush will withstand heavy pruning: both of which will almost certainly be so. Those species mentioned here are all scented.

Many acacia trees grow large, some going up to a hundred feet, but are nonetheless suitable for conservatories or sun porches in their youth. *Acacia armata*, *A. baileyana*, *A. dealbata* (syn. *A. decurrens*), *A. podalyriifolia*, *A. pubescens*, *A. retinodes* and *A. riceana* are particularly recommended; *A. × veitchiana** (known as the Exeter Hybrid), though barely scented, is a lovely 'weeping' species. There are also numerous shrubs ranging from three to six feet, such as *A. drummondii*, *A. hastulata* and *A. oxycedrus*.

Acacias should if possible be put outside from June to September: most species will withstand temperatures as low as 5° (41°F). As they root very freely, they soon use up the nutritious elements in a small pot and should therefore be fed with a fertilizer throughout the year, more frequently when the buds are starting to expand. The leaves of *A. dealbata* may turn yellow and drop if the pot is allowed to dry out or become too damp, or if the atmosphere becomes too close. (Some of the older leaves will turn yellow anyway.)

Red spider mite is the most insidious enemy of several species. *A. dealbata* and *A. × veitchiana* may also be attacked by caterpillars that weave the leaves into 'cocoons'. In general we have found these two the most tricky to adapt to indoor conditions. Propagation by seed is much easier than by cuttings (of half-ripened wood with a heel) which only take with difficulty. However germination often seems interminable because of the unusually hard seed coat. If the seeds are soaked for half an hour in dilute sulphuric acid, then washed thoroughly, they will germinate much more quickly.

* *Acacia longifolia × riceana* which arose as a seedling from *A. riceana*. (*Hillier's Manual of Trees and Shrubs*, 1972.)

Acalypha

The only species of interest to the house plant collector is *Acalypha hispida* (Red-hot Cat's Tail or Chenille Plant) which is unusual-looking with long, thick cat's tails of deep pink flowers, as Rochford and Gorer say, 'like a glorified Love-Lies-Bleeding.' It is a large shrub and plants may eventually grow up to ten feet or more.

However, it is not an easy plant because it likes a constantly high temperature and a very moist atmosphere. For most people, a plant to buy from the florist, enjoy for the flowering season and then throw away.

It is prone to mealy bug and red spider mite.

1

1. *Abutilon* 'Kentish Belle'

2. *Acacia decurrens var. dealbata*

3. *Acalypha hispida*

2

3

Achimenes

Attractive flowering pot plants that are quite widely available. *Achimenes longiflora* is the most satisfactory species; the large flat-ended tubular flowers may be blue, violet, pink or red and there is also a white variety. There are other attractive species and varieties in a wide range of colours.

If the plant is bought in flower it will go through the season very well with good light (but shading from direct sun) and plenty of moisture. When flowering is over, the plant should be put in a light, airy place to allow the rhizomes to ripen. The stem will eventually begin to yellow and the plant will die back; at this point it should be stored, dry, at a temperature of about 10° (50°F). The following February or March (depend-ing upon the availability of a temperature of about 20° (68°F)) the plant should be taken out of its pot and the small, rather delicate, scaly rhizomes – tiny leaflets bunched closely together on a stem like a young catkin – should be planted in pots with about two inches between each rhizome and a covering of three-quarters of an inch of soil.

A selective pinching out of shoots during growth will encourage bushier growth and more flowers.

Achimenes are prone to red spider but will be protected if they are given as moist an atmosphere as they like. Only a very mild insecticide should be used because the foliage is delicate.

Adiantum – see FERNS

Aechmea

osmunda

One of the most popular though least elegant of the bromeliad family. There are quite a large number of recommended species with spectacular or curious inflorescences of which the bracts are usually the most prominent feature.

The species most often offered for sale is *Aechmea fasciata* (sometimes known as *Billbergia rhodocyanea*). A full-grown plant in the house may be as much as two feet across and eighteen inches tall; the leaves are grey-green and there is a resplendent stem of sharp pointed pink bracts that enclose small blue flowers, gradually turning to pink, that peep through the layers of bract.

Aechmea fulgens has an inflorescence on a long scarlet stem consisting of numerous berry-shaped scarlet bracts enclosing small purplish-blue flowers. Then there are *A. macracantha* with wine-red foliage and red bracts enclosing the flowers, *A. mariae-reginae* with large, bright rose-pink, boat-shaped bracts; and numerous others.

The big problem with aechmeas, as with most bromeliads, is to induce flowers the second and following seasons after the plant has been bought. Elbert and Hyams quote Gowing and Leeper's experiments with the effects of betahydroxyethyl-hydrazine (BoH) on pineapples which led to the Olin Mathieson Company developing a nutrient called Omaflora that is claimed to induce blooms within a few weeks of being applied. They also quote Dr George Milstein of New York as having had success by enclosing a plant in a large polythene bag with two ripe apples for four days; we have followed this method in the case of *Tillandsia Lindeniana* with almost miraculous results.

Like many other bromeliads, aechmeas are epiphytic and in their natural conditions draw their sustenance from the water and organic matter that collect in their 'rosettes' or leaf bases. However this appears to be *faute de mieux* because Dr J. Sieber* has found that feeding through the roots gave better results than through the leaves and that a combination of both gave the best because, under greenhouse cultivation, phosphorus and potash were more fully absorbed through the roots and nitrogen through the leaves. Thus a Phostrogen solution would seem the ideal nutrient with which to water them. They should be allowed a comparatively dry 'rest period' at some point, presumably during the winter.

Thrips and scale are the pests that cause most damage to young and mature bromeliads respectively, although they do not often appear.

Propagation is usually simple as offshoots are produced abundantly. It is just a matter of severing the offshoot from the main plant with a sharp knife, dusting the wound on both plants with sulphur powder, and repotting them. It is unlikely that the parent plant will produce further flowers although it will continue to send up offshoots. Also, it may well be worth keeping for its foliage.

* Quoted by Rochford and Gorer, *The Rochford Book of Houseplants*, p. 143.

4. *Achimenes* hybrids:
   'Ambroise verschaffelt' (1)
   'Queen of Sheba' (2)
   'Paul Arnold' (3)
   'Dr Hoff' (4)
   longiflora (5)

5. *Aechmea fulgens*

6. *Aechmea fasciata*

4

5

6

Aeonium

Belonging to the Crassulaceae, aeoniums form rosettes of leaves on single or branching stems. If the plants become too straggly the rosettes may be detached and, if needed, used as cuttings. The flowers of the most interesting species are yellow or gold but other colours like greenish white or pink also occur.

Aeonium × domesticum (for which *Aichryson × domesticum* is a synonym) is mentioned by Rochford and Gorer. The main point of singling it out is that the plant gradually drops its lower leaves and gives the attractive effect of a Bonsai tree. It likes strong light and if this cannot be given it must be kept on the cool side or it will wilt.

Aeschynanthus

Less well-known perhaps than *Columnea* to which *Aeschynanthus* is closely related. These are attractive plants with deep green foliage and flowers striking in colour as well as shape.* Usually epiphytic with a climbing or straggling habit, they can therefore either be used as pot or basket plants.

When using baskets line them first with polythene then sphagnum moss and fill with a No. 1 compost. The plants need a lot of water and fertilizer and it should be remembered that baskets dry out much faster than pots. Moreover they are apt to drop their leaves and buds if the atmosphere is too dry. *Aeschynanthus lobbianus*, with scarlet and yellow flowers and attractive seed pods, is the species most usually found but there are others such as *A. grandiflorus* (deep crimson and orange flowers) and *A. speciosus* (deep orange flowers) that are equally fine.

* The Royal Horticultural Society's *Dictionary of Gardening* mentions the 'agreeable fragrance' of *Aeschynanthus* but these are quite a few around that lack it.

Agave

A genus rather similar to the *Aloe*, though belonging to the New World. The long spiny, often succulent leaves have formal appeal but agaves are slow growers and it takes a number of years before the green or brownish flowers appear, though not a hundred, which belief led to the name Century Plant.

The smallest and hence the most practical species are *Agave albicans*, *A. filifera*, *A. parviflora* and *A. victoriae-reginae* although, even of these, the flower spikes can be very tall.

Agaves are tough plants and will benefit by being stood outside during the summer.

Aglaonema

Useful foliage plants which grow well in a certain amount of shade. Leaves are about nine inches long, various shades of green, usually with markings of another shade or white.

They benefit from frequent spraying and high humidity.

Aichryson – see AEONIUM

7. *Aeonium domesticum variegatum*

8. *Aeschynanthus lobbianus*

9. *Agave victoriae-americanae*

10. *Aglaonema* 'Silver Queen'

7

8

9

10

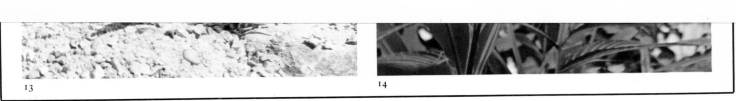

13

14

Allamanda

Allamanda cathartica with its clusters of large bright yellow trumpet-shaped flowers is the most exotic climbing plant that is widely offered for sale, thanks to the enterprise of some

the plant will wilt badly if subjected to temperatures much over 25° (77°F) unless the atmosphere can be kept both airy and humid. The only recourse if the temperature is high and

Amaryllis

Though *Amaryllis belladonna* is related to the daffodil the beautiful fragrant flowers resemble those of a trumpet lily. Several rosy pink flowers are produced at the top of a two-foot stalk, sometimes during the winter.

A. belladonna is hardy in warmer gardens but when grown indoors, as pot plants, the long large bulbs should be treated in the same way as hippeastrums (q.v.), the bulbs usually sold as 'amaryllis'.

Amomum *cardamomum* – see ELETTARIA *cardamomum*

Angraecum – see ORCHIDS

Anthurium

The spectacular appearance of an anthurium in flower with the spadix projecting sharply from a (usually) brilliant red, flat, shiny spathe will attract some and repel others. The flowers are usually well set off by handsome foliage.

There are numerous species, as well as hybrids, and it is best to choose a plant in flower because the flowers will last well

but are by no means easy to produce.

Plants need a very moist atmosphere with plenty of water and good drainage.

Propagation is by seed, or by division; if the latter, great care should be taken not to damage the rather fragile roots.

Aphelandra

Aphelandras are nature's perfect gift to the plastic plant purveyor. If they had not existed he would not have dared invent them. However some may not be repelled by them and may even find them effective when one or more plants are included in a group, predominantly of evergreens. The leaves are a shiny green and, in the forms most usually sold, variegated with creamy white. The flowers fan out from a central spike and are usually yellow, orange or scarlet.

Aphelandra squarrosa, and its varieties with yellow flowers and orange or red bracts, is the species most frequently met with but *A. fascinator* with scarlet flowers, *A. chamissoniana*

(yellow) and *A. margaritae* (orange or yellow) are also recommended.

Aphelandras should be given a lot of light and moisture until they begin to flower, when they will last longer if kept in a drier atmosphere.

Once they have flowered they may have to be thrown away because they are too difficult to carry through a winter and bring again into flower without greenhouse or conservatory conditions.

Aralia

Many plants originally in this genus have now been reclassified under different genera. Those that we describe are to be found as follows:

Aralia elegantissima – see *Dizygotheca elegantissima*
A. japonica – see *Fatsia japonica*
A. schefflera – see *Schefflera digitata*
A. sieboldii – see *Fatsia japonica*

11. *Allamanda cathartica*

12. *Allophyton mexicanum*

13. *Aloe variegata*

14. *Alpinia speciosa*

11

12

13

14

Amaryllis

Though *Amaryllis belladonna* is related to the daffodil the beautiful fragrant flowers resemble those of a trumpet lily. Several rosy pink flowers are produced at the top of a two-foot stalk, sometimes during the winter.

A. belladonna is hardy in warmer gardens but when grown indoors, as pot plants, the long large bulbs should be treated in the same way as hippeastrums (q.v.), the bulbs usually sold as 'amaryllis'.

Amomum *cardamomum* – see ELETTARIA *cardamomum*

Angraecum – see ORCHIDS

Anthurium

osmunda
+
No. I

The spectacular appearance of an anthurium in flower with the spadix projecting sharply from a (usually) brilliant red, flat, shiny spathe will attract some and repel others. The flowers are usually well set off by handsome foliage.

There are numerous species, as well as hybrids, and it is best to choose a plant in flower because the flowers will last well

but are by no means easy to produce.

Plants need a very moist atmosphere with plenty of water and good drainage.

Propagation is by seed, or by division; if the latter, great care should be taken not to damage the rather fragile roots.

Aphelandra

Aphelandras are nature's perfect gift to the plastic plant purveyor. If they had not existed he would not have dared invent them. However some may not be repelled by them and may even find them effective when one or more plants are included in a group, predominantly of evergreens. The leaves are a shiny green and, in the forms most usually sold, variegated with creamy white. The flowers fan out from a central spike and are usually yellow, orange or scarlet.

Aphelandra squarrosa, and its varieties with yellow flowers and orange or red bracts, is the species most frequently met with but *A. fascinator* with scarlet flowers, *A. chamissoniana*

(yellow) and *A. margaritae* (orange or yellow) are also recommended.

Aphelandras should be given a lot of light and moisture until they begin to flower, when they will last longer if kept in a drier atmosphere.

Once they have flowered they may have to be thrown away because they are too difficult to carry through a winter and bring again into flower without greenhouse or conservatory conditions.

Aralia

Many plants originally in this genus have now been re-classified under different genera. Those that we describe are to be found as follows:

Aralia elegantissima – see *Dizygotheca elegantissima*
A. japonica – see *Fatsia japonica*
A. schefflera – see *Schefflera digitata*
A. sieboldii – see *Fatsia japonica*

15

15. *Amaryllis belladonna*

16. *Anthurium andreanum*

17. *Aphelandra squarrosa louisae*

16

17

Araucaria

Araucaria excelsa, the Norfolk Island Pine, is perhaps the most satisfactory species, for growing indoors, of a genus that includes *A. araucana* (the Monkey Puzzle tree). It will eventually grow up to two hundred feet but young plants with their symmetrical, dense, awl-shaped leaves have formal decorative beauty.

Ardisia

A useful plant because there is usually something happening: the foliage is evergreen, the clusters of flowers are red, pink, white or purple and the fruit (berries), which may last throughout the winter until the next flowering, is usually bright red, though in some species black.

Ardisia crispa, *A. japonica* and *A. mamillata* are three recommended species.

When the shrub is some eighteen inches to two feet high it is at its best. Early the next spring, let the roots dry a little, then cut the plant back to within two inches of the soil, start watering again and good new growth will form. The soil should be slightly acid.

Aregelia - see NEOREGELIA

Argyroderma – see under MESEMBRYANTHEMUM

Aristolochia

These exotic, rampant climbers are conservatory, not house plants and are such vigorous growers that they have to be kept ruthlessly in check even there. If you have a pillar or suchlike a plant is best twined spirally round it with the strands at two-inch intervals. Otherwise some form of trellis is essential.

The flowers of most species are an extraordinary shape, like orchids run amok, and in some cases have a disagreeable scent.

It is best to choose one that is evergreen rather than deciduous. *Aristolochia elegans*, the Calico Plant, with curious cup-shaped flowers, purplish-brown, veined with yellow or white is the most common but is deciduous, as is *A. brasiliensis* (purple with darker markings). *A. odoratissima* (with *pleasantly* scented purple flowers) and *A. ringens* (with huge pale green flowers marked with blackish purple) are on the other hand evergreen and are among those well worth cultivating.

The foliage is prone to attacks of insects, particularly red spider mite.

Arum

Should not be confused with the larger and more spectacular Arum Lily, *Zantedeschia aethiopica*. Arums are quite attractive plants both for their flowers and their foliage. *Arum italicum marmoratum* (marbled leaves and bright berries), *A. orientale* (deep purple spathe) and *A. palaestinum* (purple spathe) are perhaps the best species.

For cultivation see *Zantedeschia*.

18. *Araucaria excelsa*

19. *Ardisia crispa*

20. *Aristolochia elegans*

21 *Arum creticum*

18

19

20

21

Asparagus

The flowers are inconspicuous but the filmy leaves are delicately attractive and the plant will carry berries throughout most of the winter. *Asparagus madagascariensis* with red berries, *A. plumosus*, blackish berries, and *A. sprengeri*, a climber with bright red berries that is particularly good for use in hanging baskets, are recommended. *A. meyeri*, a densely tufted species, is also outstandingly decorative and well suited to hanging baskets.

Aspidistra

An imposing evergreen that will stand a deal of neglect although in fact it likes plenty of moisture and will respond to care by giving shiny dark leaves free of disfiguring brown tips.

Aspidistra lurida, with leaves up to twenty inches long, is the most handsome species; it also has a variegated form.

Asplenium – see FERNS

Azalea – see RHODODENDRON

Bambusa

If you have enough space and an appropriate style of decoration – *fin de siècle* or modern – some species of Bamboo can be most effective.

The genus ranges from fully tropical species such as *B. arundinacea* and *B. vulgaris* to *B. glaucescens* which originates, apparently, in China and Japan. *B. glaucescens* and its varieties are probably the best in our context as they can be tough plants as well as relatively manageable.

There are many related genera.

Bauera

An unobtrusive little evergreen shrub, *Bauera rubioides*, the best species, has pale red, pink or white drooping flowers which appear almost throughout the year.

Baueras are lime haters but otherwise easy to cultivate. Prune after flowering if the plant becomes straggly. Does not need much fertilizer.

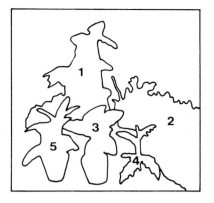

22. *Asparagus plumosus* (1), *A. sprengeri* (2), also
    Calathea zebrina (3), *Gynura aurantiaca* (purple
    form) (4), *Setreasea purpurea* (5)

23. *Aspidistra lurida variegata*

24. *Bambusa sinobambusa tootskik*

25. *Bauera rubioides* (white form)

22

23

24

25

Bauhinia

Delightfully graceful shrubs, trees, or climbers, mostly with smooth, delicate green kidney-shaped leaves of the texture of some eucalyptus and with racemes of equally delicate flowers with long, flowing, separated petals.

It is hard to choose which species to recommend. *Bauhinia corymbosa* has pinkish petals; *B. galpinii* has scarlet, *B. acuminata* white, *B. purpurea* shades of pink with white and *B. tomentosa* pale yellow with a brown or red splodge at the base.

These plants have the usual tropical requirements and will flourish quite well with plenty of light. They are worth becoming more widely known.

Cuttings need moisture as well as bottom heat to root. They should have their leaves removed. They are not easy to deal with. Seeds are perhaps a better bet, although they too have their hazards, perhaps the greatest being a tendency to rot before germinating. This is likely to be due to the condition in which the seeds have been received by the seedsman and is not necessarily his fault.

Begonia

If you like begonias you are lucky because there is no genus of plants so suitable for indoor cultivation that offers such a variety of colour and size in flower and leaf. Moreover, if you concentrate on begonias you can easily choose from among the nine hundred or so species a group of some half dozen that will give you an array of flowers and decorative foliage throughout the year.

Those who specialize or want to do so will of course go to monographs on the subject. This entry, as others, is written for the non-specialist or as a preliminary guide for the novitiate.

Certain general principles can be applied to the cultivation of all begonias. They are sensitive to over- and under-watering. They must, therefore, be planted in porous soil which is kept well-drained but moist during their active period. To flower well begonias need plenty of light but the possibility of scorching from the direct rays of the sun must be avoided. Temperatures should be about 20° (68°F) to induce flowering but should be lower once the plant is in bloom: ideally, below 15° (59°F). They need a balanced fertilizer during the active period: every four weeks, not more.

Once this has been said, it is essential to divide begonias into groups to produce some order out of the variety of habit and appearance.

The Royal Horticultural Society's *Dictionary of Gardening* divides them into four groups:
I *Bulbous or almost* so, which contains only the winter-flowering species, *B. socotrana*;
II *Tuberous*;
III *Rhizomatous* which includes the *B. rex* type;
IV *Fibrous-rooted*.

Group I should really be regarded as a one-season plant unless you have a heated greenhouse or conservatory.

Group II contains some outstanding summer- and winter-flowering species. When flowering is over the plant should be dried off and, as soon as the leaves have dropped, the stems should be gradually twisted off the tuber and discarded. The tubers should then be stored in a cool, frost-proof place; if space is a problem, they can be taken out of their pots and stored in boxes of dry peat or fibre. No light is necessary.

In February or March for the summer- and May or June (or later if you have growth lamps) for the winter-flowering species, start the plants up again in a temperature of 15–20° (59–68°F) under the general conditions described above.

Group III contains primarily *B. rex* and others of a similar type that are valued above all for their foliage. They, too, have a dormant period in the winter and should then be allowed almost to dry out. Continue to syringe, however, and the plants will again come to life.

Group IV. This is the largest group and contains numerous coveted species, varieties and hybrids that flower mainly in the summer but also in winter, among them some elegant tall, woody species, such as *B. corallina*. They have their dormant period after the flowering season (which can last for several months) and may be kept in their pots for another season. However, they tend not to be so good during the second season and as they are easily raised from seed to full flower in six months this is the best course for the 'home-grower'; otherwise throw them away and visit the nurseryman when you want some more.

The table below gives a selection of species for each season with the emphasis on the winter, when there is less competition from other flowers and begonias are that much more welcome (although there is a far greater selection available during the summer). When the flowering period of a species extends over two seasons it will be listed under both columns (it should, as always, be remembered that such 'seasons' cannot be wholly depended on as plants react differently to different treatment

26. *Bauhinia variegata* var. *candida*

27. *Bauhinia tomentosa*

28. *Begonia boliviensis*

29. *Begonia tuberhybrida* 'Buttermilk'

26

27

28

29

and surroundings). Against each species the R.H.S. Group number is given. A fifth column gives a selection of the *B. rex* type (R.H.S. Group III) – valued chiefly for their foliage, as stated above.

Begonias may be afflicted by fungus disease, a powdery mil-dew, and if so should be treated with dinocap or thiram. They may also be attacked by vine weevil and leaf eelworm: vine weevil will cause wilting and may be stopped by gamma-BHC. Leaf eelworm may be eliminated by a drenching of thionazin.

Spring	Summer	Autumn	Winter	Foliage
	+*B.baumannii II* * *B. boliviensis II*			
		B. cathayana IV	*B.* × *carrierei IV*	
* *B.convolvulacea III*		+*B.conchifolia III*		
B.corallina IV ——————				
+*B.cyclophylla II*				
	B.davisii II			*B.daedalea III* *B.decora III*
	B. × *erfordia IV* *B.evansiana II*			
		B. froebelii II————————		
B. fuchsioides IV			*B. fuchsioides IV*	
	+*B.fulgens II* *B.glaucophylla III*			
B.hemsleyana IV ————				*B.heracleifolia III*
			B.incarnata IV	*B.imperialis III*
B. × *lucerna IV* ————				
			B.lyncheana II *B.natalensis II*	*B.masoniana III*
B.nitida IV————				
+*B.nitida IV var. odorata*				
B. polyantha IV			*B.polyantha IV*	
	B.semperflorens IV ————			*B. rex III*
		B.socotrana I————		

* *suitable for hanging baskets*
+ *scented*

Beloperone

Beloperone guttata or the Shrimp Plant has the double advantage of being easy to grow and having a long flowering season. Thus if you like the look of the plant – brownish-rose coloured bracts, shaped like shrimps, enclose small white, red, purple or blue flowers – you are unlikely to be disappointed.

You can prune it at any time to keep it from straggling.

Beloperone guttata is the synonym of *Drejerella guttata* but the name used here is so well established that it was thought better to keep to it.

Billbergia

A genus of terrestrial and almost hardy bromeliads. *Billbergia nutans* is the species most usually offered and has curious pink-green-and-blue bell-shaped flowers hanging from a spike with long pointed pink bracts. *B.* × *windii* is a cross between *B. decora* and *B. nutans* and is perhaps more striking.

Much the easiest genus of the bromeliads and there is no difficulty to induce them to flower. Otherwise, see *Aechmea*.

Blechnum – see FERNS

30. *Begonia socotrana* 'Mrs Leopold de Rothschild'

31. *Begonia rex* 'Merry Christmas'

32. *Beloperone guttata*

33. *Billbergia nutans*

30

31

32

33

Boronia

Boronias belong to the same family as citrus plants (although to the amateur they have little resemblance) and are much admired in their native Australia.

The flowers of most species range from deep rose through pink to white and are often beautifully scented. Moreover they will flower in the winter. Unfortunately plants are not easily come by and the only species at all widely available is *Boronia megastigma*, a delightful plant with numerous quite small cup-shaped flowers of a purplish brown colour outside (unusual for this genus) and tinged with yellow inside; they have a lovely scent.

The snag about boronias is that they like plenty of moisture and a much cooler atmosphere than the great majority of house plants. They do best within a temperature range of 10–15° (50–59°F) although they will tolerate higher temperatures.

Although we have proposed a No. 1 soil mix, boronias are used to a high percentage of sand in the soil and Rochford and Gorer recommend a simple mixture of sand and peat.* They dislike lime.

Plants can be pruned immediately after flowering.

Like citruses, boronias are prone to attacks of scale insects.

Half-ripened lateral shoots should be used for cuttings. They should have slight bottom heat but otherwise be kept at about 10° (50°F).

* *The Rochford Book of Flowering Pot Plants*, p. 74.

Bougainvillea

For many of those who react to an atmosphere of flowers bougainvilleas, together with 'mimosas' (*Acacia*) and plumbago, call up the blue skies and sun of southern Europe, above all of the Mediterranean Riviera, or, in the U.S.A., of the Caribbean, California or Florida. Although we cannot hope to achieve indoors the luxuriant abundance of any of these plants that we see farther south it is hard to resist the temptation to bring a patch of Southern nostalgia into the house.

Bougainvilleas are among the 'showiest' plants in existence. They are vigorous climbers and the great tresses, usually of bright purple, trained against houses in hot countries or hanging down from walls automatically attract the eye. The colour comes from the bracts which almost enclose the tiny flowers inside.

Apart from the most usual *Bougainvilliea glabra* or *B. spectabilis*, there are numerous more delicately or excitingly coloured varieties or hybrids and experiment is constantly continuing. The varieties *cypheri* and *sanderiana* of *B. glabra* are a softer, more delicate colour; then there is the striking cinnabar-coloured hybrid *B.* 'Lindleyana', the lovely deep yellow *B.* × *millari*, the crimson turning to magenta *B.* × *buttiana* and there are numerous other hybrids.

Bougainvilleas are not very easy plants to maintain in flower in the house. (In their second and subsequent years they are likely to give a better display than when just bought from a florist.) When being brought to flower the plants need maximum light, a temperature of around 20–25° (68–77°F), and plenty of moisture. When the bracts are in full colour a cooler atmosphere will make them last longer but the main task is to ensure that the temperature does not outstrip the moisture or the flowers will dry at the last joint of the stem and the bracts will fall.

Plants are best bought when the bracts are formed but before the flowers have opened. Examine the tiny flower buds carefully to see that they are full and not at all shrivelled. You will thus ensure a flowering season of at least a month and with luck throughout the summer. During the winter temperatures and moisture should be reduced and when the plants re-awaken in the spring they may be pruned to maintain a convenient size. They are quite likely to shed their leaves in the winter.

Watch for signs of red spider, aphis, scale insects and mealy bug.

34

35

36

34. *Boronia alata*

35. *Boronia heterophylla*

36. *Bougainvillea* mixed:
   B. glabra (1)
   B. 'Alexandra Purple' (2)
   B. 'Killie Campbell' (3)
   B. millari (4)

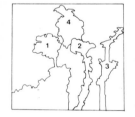

Bouvardia

These are most attractive evergreen plants with the advantage that they can produce a mass of jasmine-like flowers during the autumn or winter. *Bouvardia humboldtii*, *B. jasminiflora* and *B. longiflora* are particularly recommended because they are scented. The flowers of each of these species are white. *B. triphylla* has striking orange-scarlet flowers but they are not scented.

If cuttings are wanted, the plants should be cut back after flowering and the new shoots should be nipped off when they are about two inches long and given bottom heat under glass of 20–25° (68–77°F) or a little more.

Breynia

The appeal of *Breynia nivosa*, a delicately attractive shrub commonly known as the Snow Bush, lies in the beautiful markings of its smallish oval leaves in green and white, rather than the flowers which are insignificant. Its varieties also have attractive leaves: those of *atropurpurea* gradually turn from

dark green to deep purple and those of *roseopicta*, perhaps the most beautiful of all, are green and white delicately suffused with pink, darkening to wine red.

B. nivosa is synonymous with *Phyllanthus nivosus*.

Browallia

Although some species are perennial browallias are usually regarded as annuals but they have a long flowering season and their numerous violet blue (or white) flowers make a delightful display. *Browallia speciosa* or *B. viscosa* are the most beautiful species.

If you plan to raise plants from seed yourself (rather than buying them) the seeds should be sown in a standard seed compost under glass with the temperature about 15° (59°F).

If flowers are wanted during the summer the seeds should be sown during March but if they are wanted in the winter or spring they should be sown some time from July to September. Thin the seedlings out at the earliest convenient moment and later transfer them to individual pots; three per pot is often recommended for this plant, in 3-inch, then 5-inch, pots. *B. speciosa* will give more abundant flowers if the shoots are pinched out several times.

Brunfelsia

Attractive, exotic evergreen shrubs with plentiful single flowers at various times of the year.

Brunfelsia americana has flowers in June that are white at first, then yellow and strongly scented, especially at night. *B. latifolia*, whose flowers are lavender, gradually turning to white, is also very fragrant and flowers in the winter-early spring. *B. calycina* is like *B. latifolia* except that the flowers start darker and are unscented. *B. bonodora* (Yesterday, Today and Tomorrow) has smaller flowers in great profusion that are delightfully scented.

High humidity is essential, or the tips of the leaves will die

and become unsightly and the buds (and leaves) will start to drop.

Brunfelsia may need to be potted on every two years and can be pruned just after flowering to maintain an attractive shape; *B. bonodora* is a very vigorous grower and will certainly need to be both pruned and potted on frequently. It is more demanding of humidity than *B. calycina*.

Propagation is by cuttings of half ripened wood, in a sandy soil at about 20° (68°F). Again, high humidity is essential and a propagator is required. Hardening off of the rooted plants must be very gradual.

37. *Bouvardia humboldtii*

38. *Breynia nivosa*

39. *Browallia speciosa* 'Major'

40. *Brunfelsia calycina* 'Macrantha'

37

38

39

40

Bryophyllum – see KALANCHOE

Bulbs

There is a group of bulbs, all of which will grow well outside as spring bulbs but which can be grown indoors and thus give immense pleasure through their form, colour and often scent as well as being delightful reminders that spring will eventually come.

The bulbs, corms or tubers usually treated in this way are crocus, hyacinths and narcissi but some irises and tulips as well as *Chionodoxa*, *Fritillaria meleagris*, *Galanthus* (snowdrops), *Muscari* and scillas are also rewarding.

Such bulbs give the best results if they are treated like temperate zone house plants and are planted in a No. 3 compost in pots with good drainage. They can however be raised in containers without drainage in which case they must be planted in bulb fibre or placed on a base of pebbles and charcoal with water added. Charcoal should not be left out because it performs the important function of keeping the medium sweet. When either of the first two methods are used the bulbs should be two-thirds covered with the medium which should first have been thoroughly soaked with water. In the third case the bottom of the bulbs should be fractionally above the surface of the water so that the roots can develop without the body of the bulbs being immersed, to avoid the danger of rot.

Whichever method is adopted the bulbs can be planted at any point from August to the end of October for flowering from November until the end of February. When planted the bulbs should be sprinkled to a depth of an inch with dry fibre or peat and put in a well ventilated cool place, *not* in a dark airless cupboard. They should be inspected once a week during the first month to ensure that the conditions are right and thereafter once a month to see that the medium is moist or that the level of the water is correct, until the leaf buds have started to form. They should then be moved to an equally cool place with moderate light; if this place is too warm the leaves will develop at the expense of the roots and subsequently the flowers.

They should be kept in their new location until the flower buds are clearly visible, at which point they should be moved into full light and a temperature of 15–20° (59–68°F). When the flowers are about to come out the bulbs can be moved to a position with less light but the closer to 15° that they can be kept the longer they will last. Meanwhile the medium should be kept moist and the atmosphere as humid as possible. If the 'pebbles and water' method has been used the bulbs will benefit at this stage from having the water-level topped up with correctly diluted nutrient but when the other mediums are used it is best to keep off nutrient because the bulbs will get all that they need from their own resources and the medium; if over-fed they may grow inordinately and develop leaves at the expense of flowers.

When the flowers are over, the bulbs can be moved to an inconspicuous position but should be kept growing until the leaves start to yellow and die back. Then they can be dried off and stored for planting outdoors in the autumn. It is advisable always to buy new bulbs (and the best that you can afford) for indoor cultivation. Bulbs kept indoors for a second year are rarely as good as the first and, in particular, those that have been specially prepared for forcing will have lost that property.

The choice of bulbs for growing indoors must obviously be a matter of personal taste. All hyacinths are suitable for this treatment and Roman hyacinths are particularly easy to bring on early as they are very quick growers. All crocuses too are likely to be easy. There are some particularly delightful, delicately coloured miniature hybrids of *Crocus chrysanthus* such as 'Warley White', 'Zwanenburg Bronze' and 'Gipsy Girl'; *Crocus fleischeri* and cultivars of *Crocus vernus* are also beautiful. (The last species is not easily available.) In the case of narcissi and tulips there are hybrids that respond particularly well to indoor treatment and others that are best avoided. It is therefore essential to follow the advice of a reputable bulb supplier.

Butia – see PALMS

41. *Chionodoxa sardensis*

42. *Hyacinthus Cynthella* 'The Bride'

43. *Iris reticulata* 'Cantab'

44. *Narcissus juncifolius*

41

42

43

44

Cacti

Perhaps more than most categories of plants, cacti (and some succulents) are apt to rouse extreme emotions, on the one hand of delight and fascination, on the other of boredom or revulsion. For this and for other reasons cacti are liable to come within the province solely of collectors and specialists and, except for the occasional epiphyllum or Christmas Cactus, to be ignored by the general house plant enthusiast, which is a pity because a lot of pleasure can be derived from even a small group of cacti as part of a heterogeneous collection of plants.

Potential collectors are advised to start with one of the excellent introductions to the cultivation of cacti and other succulents*. As well as being authoritative and lucid introductions to the subject these books contain much useful, detailed information and excellent photographs of a large number of cacti, etc.

What follows must, within the scope of this book, be brief and elementary. If the reader is encouraged to try his hand and is not misled the purpose will be achieved.

The first point to settle is: what is a cactus? The cactus family consists of some two hundred genera and thousands of species. In botanical terms Cactaceae are distinguished from other families through having organs, unique to themselves, called 'areoles' which are 'cushions' produced in the leaf axils (or where the leaves would have been) that bear 'spines and frequently wool, felt, bristles and hairs'. This is the only quality that distinguishes them from other succulents.**

Because of the size of the family it has been divided into three 'tribes', or groups, and a number of 'sub-tribes'.*** The tribes are:

1. Pereskieae, which consist of tall spiny shrubs with leaves and need not concern us here.

2. Opuntieae. All the plants in this family have spines and also 'glochids' which are very fine tufts of bristles on the areoles that embed themselves in the skin when touched and come away from the plant.

3. Cereeae. This tribe contains all the rest of the cacti and is distinguished negatively from the other two by having neither leaves nor glochids.

* Ginn's *Cacti and other Succulents*, London, 1963, E. & B. Lamb's *Pocket Encyclopaedia of Cacti in Colour, including other Succulents*, London, 1969 and New York, 1970, Van Ness' *Cacti and Succulents for Home and Garden*, New York, 1971, or Sunset Editors' *Succulents and Cactus*, California, 1970.

** For other succulents covered in this book, see *Aeonium, Aloe, Ceropegia, Cotyledon, Crassula, Echeveria, Euphorbia tirucalii, Gasteria, Haworthia, Kalanchoe, Mesembryanthemum, Rochea, Sedum, Sempervivum* and *Stapelia*.

*** Britton and Rose, *The Cactaceae*, 1923. This is followed by Ginns, op. cit. E. & B. Lamb have evolved a slightly different system of grouping, op. cit., pp. 45–7.

A possible misconception should perhaps be cleared up immediately. One is apt to think of cacti as inhabiting exclusively arid, scorching desert areas. Most of them do but there are some important genera within the tribe cereeae, such as *Epiphyllum*, *Nopalxochia* and *Schlumbergera* that live in tropical rain forests and are epiphytic; there are other partially epiphytic climbing cacti, rooted in the ground, from similar regions but these are scarcely practical for indoor conditions.

Of the epiphytic cacti, in terms of house plants, the epiphyllum hybrids hold a dominant position. These are mostly hybrids of *Epiphyllum ackermannii* with some of the large flowered upright cacti. The elongated, curiously shaped flat green leaves of most of them (like rolled-out dough) may be an acquired taste but it is one worth acquiring because of the lovely large flowers that these plants produce in many delicate shades of colour and sometimes delightfully fragrant. Some of them are rather slow or infrequent flowerers but others are quite abundant. Of the easier epiphyllums that are also scented, *E. cooperii* (white inner and yellow outer petals), *E. oxypetalum* (white flowers), and *E. wrayii* (white, yellow backed petals) can be particularly recommended. Other epiphytes worth noting are *Rhipsalidopsis gaertneri* (syn. *Schlumbergera gaertneri*), the Whitsun Cactus, *Rhipsalidopsis rosea*, the Easter Cactus, and *Schlumbergera truncata* (syn. *Zygocactus truncatus*), the Christmas Cactus – whose popular names indicate their flowering times.

These cacti are quite easy to cultivate. They should be planted in a No. 3 mix and particular attention should be paid to the drainage. They should in fact be treated like other house plants from the rainy tropics and given plenty of light and moisture during the active season. Thereafter they should be kept dry and cool but in a light, airy position. The 'active' treatment should be started at the first sign of new growth. Some of these cacti produce flower buds in great abundance, some of which will be cast off naturally but as the buds turn towards the source of light the plants should not be moved at this stage or the process will be aggravated.

The rest of the cactus family belonging to the opuntieae and cereeae tribes conforms more closely to the conventional view of what a 'cactus' is.

It would be going into too much detail to list the sub-tribes or the genera that comprise them. On the assumption that the beginner would like to have a majority of cacti that flower combined with one or two that are remarkable for their shape, it is suggested that a start is made with certain of the smaller cacti (in general the smaller the ultimate size of a cactus the sooner it will flower: many of the dwarf cacti will flower the year after they have been propagated). Ginns suggests first the *Mammillaria* which is a large genus of small plants with many species and hybrids to choose from. *Mammillaria gracilis* and *M. cowperae* have yellow flowers; *M. mendelliana* has pink flowers against a background of white fluff; *M. karwinskiana* has cream flowers and *M. wildii* has white flowers. *M. bocasana* has yellowish flowers and produces curious, elongated, tubular, pink, edible fruit. The rebutias which Ginns also recommends have perhaps more striking flowers, particularly *Rebutia aureiflora* with orange yellow flowers, *R. marsoneri* (yellow),

45

45· *Chamaecereus silvestrii*

46. *Cacti* mixed, including: *Mammillaria*
(foreground) *Rebutia* (centre) *Opuntia* (rear)

46

R. pygmaea (rosy-purple), etc. Others to be recommended are *Astrophytum* (large yellow flowers), *Chamaecereus* (orange and scarlet), *Coryphantha*, *Lobivia*, *Notocactus*; and a special plea for *Echinopsis* which has large, long usually white and sometimes fragrant tubular flowers: *Echinopsis turbinata* strongly scented (white) and *E. multiplex* also scented (pale pink). For shape, *Cereus chalybaeus*, *Espostoa lanata* or some species of *Trichocereus* are suggested.

The general guide-lines for the cultivation of these cacti are:

1. **Soil.** The recommended mix is:

$\frac{1}{3}$ loam
$\frac{1}{3}$ sharp sand
$\frac{1}{3}$ leaf mould or peat

The Lambs recommend that to each gallon of soil should be added:

4 heaped teaspoons of bone meal
3 heaped teaspoons of gypsum
1 heaped teaspoon of superphosphate

The pots must be provided with good drainage with crocks. Ginns recommends adding paradichlorobenzene as a preventative of root mealy bugs. He also recommends that plants should be re-potted every year.

2. **Watering.** With the opuntieae and the non-epiphytic cereeae it is much better to err on the side of under- than of over-watering; obviously enough such cacti can survive long periods of drought without irreparable damage. Too much water on the other hand will produce an unhealthy look in the plant and, particularly when it is inactive, the possiblity of root rot. In general the best method in the active period is to give the plants a soaking, wait until they have just – but only just – dried out then repeat the process, and so on. The interval between watering may be as little as a day or as much as a week or more, depending on the size of the pots, the heat and the atmosphere. Throughout the dormant periods the plants should be kept almost dry.

3. **Light and Air.** The majority of cacti (and all those mentioned here) will do best with as much concentrated light during the day as can be provided. They must however have a period of darkness and, like other plants, should have the daylight extended artificially as little as possible. The opuntieae and the non-epiphytic cereeae thrive in a clear, dry atmosphere and dislike both humidity and draughts. Although they dislike humidity they benefit from a light spraying at night, during the active season, which corresponds to the dew to which they are used and helps the bud formation.

4. **Temperature.** The majority of cacti will fare best in a maximum temperature of 25° (77°F) during the active season and a minimum of 10° (50°F) during the inactive season. It is best to avoid a higher 'inactive' temperature than this because otherwise the plants will not in fact be inactive and their strength will be dissipated.

So much for the conditions for successful cultivation.

There are also the inevitable hazards that happen even to the best treated plants. Mealy bugs are apt to attack and be hidden in awkward crevices and there is a root mealy bug that is easier to prevent (as suggested: by mixing paradichlorobenzene into the potting soil) than to detect. Scale insects may appear and, because of the drier atmosphere that should be surrounding cacti, red spider mite can be particularly active. These pests can be countered by the usual remedies but if the cacti have other succulents such as Crassulaceae mixed in with them care should be taken not to use an insecticide that will damage the Crassulaceae.

As to diseases, the only ones that are at all common are stem and root rot. Stem rot should be visible to the naked eye and root rot can be suspected from a generally unhealthy appearance in a plant. Treatment is to cut away the affected parts, dust with sulphur powder or suchlike and allow the plant to dry out before starting to water again.

Propagation of cacti is quite easy, whether by seed, by offset, or by cuttings which should be dried out before planting until they have calloused and then watered only very sparingly until they have rooted. It is also relatively easy to achieve results with grafting but that is outside the scope of this book.

Caesalpinia

A genus of trees of which some species make striking house plants when young. The foliage and flowers look somewhat like those of *Cassia auricularis*.

Caesalpinia pulcherrima has racemes of small orange-red flowers with long, tuft-like stamens; in *C. vernalis* the flowers are yellow with a scarlet blotch.

Cuttings are difficult to root. They should be on the soft side and have bottom heat. Seed or layering are more reliable.

47

49

47. *Epiphyllum ackermannii*

48. *Cacti* and
    other succulents:
    Ariocarpus fissuratus (1)
    A. kotschubeyanus (2)
    Cephalocereus senilis (3)
    Conophytum species (4)
    Crassula arborescens (5)
    Echeveria *species* (6)
    E. gibbiflora (7)
    Echinocereus species (8)
    Hamatocactus setispinus (9)
    Kalanchoe beharensis (10)
    Lithops species (11)
    Oreocereus celsianus (12)
    Pleiospilos species (13)
    Schlumbergera truncata (14)

49. *Caesalpinia japonica*

48

Caladium

Plants valued for the striking appearance of their begonia-like foliage. The species are very variable and most plants to be found are anyhow hybrids, chiefly from *Caladium bicolor*, although *C. picturatum* and *C. schomburgkii* have also provided their share. The heart-shaped leaves may be orange-red, red or, in *C. candidum*, white with prominent green veins: this last has particularly handsome foliage.

Caladiums need plenty of light to bring out the markings but shade from direct strong sun, and plenty of water during growth but good drainage.

Unfortunately for the house plant collector, caladiums have a dormant period in the winter when they shed their leaves. The tubers must then be kept only just moist.

Calathea

Calatheas belong to the family Marantaceae and are frequently confused with marantas which they closely resemble. There are about a hundred species among which are some of the most striking foliage plants. The oblong, usually smooth, leaves generally have patterns in various shades of green and white on a green silvery base; the underside of the leaves is often reddish or purple. There are insignificant spikes of flowers.

A number of species are offered for sale. Among them, *Calathea ornata*, *C. picturata* and *C. zebrina* are admired for their exquisitely coloured foliage. But perhaps the most remarkable are *C. backemiana* and *C. mackoyana* that give the impression of having had a primitive painting of a leafed plant stencilled on the silver-green background of their leaves.

In general calatheas need tropical conditions to flourish. The temperature should not be allowed much below 15° (59°F) and in the growing season should go up to 25° (77°F) or more. A high degree of humidity is essential but the drainage must be good.

Plants should be re-potted annually at any time from July until spring, or the foliage will become too cramped to develop attractively. At the same time plants can be propagated by careful division of the roots.

Calathea zebrina is illustrated with *Asparagus*, plate 22.

Calceolaria

Calceolarias seem to arouse quite strong opposing sentiments. Their strange rather gaudy pouch- or slipper-like flowers either repel or appeal.

Although yellow predominates in the species, flowers may be had in a number of colours; and there is usually a spotting of a second colour – brown, purple or black on the base colour. There are both small- and large-flowered species. *Calceolaria integrifolia*, with a mass of small yellow flowers, is a species to be recommended and there are the numerous large-flowered hybrids of *C. multiflora*.

Calceolarias are best raised from seed but this has to be done during the early part of June to flower the following year and so is only really practicable if you have a conservatory or greenhouse. Otherwise they may be bought as growing plants during the summer in which they are wanted and treated as annuals, although some of the shrubby forms should be kept from year to year.

The plants should be watched for green fly to which they are prone and for leaf eelworm which will reveal itself through brown or yellow patches on the leaves; thionazin is the best remedy. They may also be infected with the virus disease, spotted wilt, in which case the plant should be destroyed.

50

50. *Caladium* hybrids

51. *Calceolaria* × *multiflora* 'Nana'

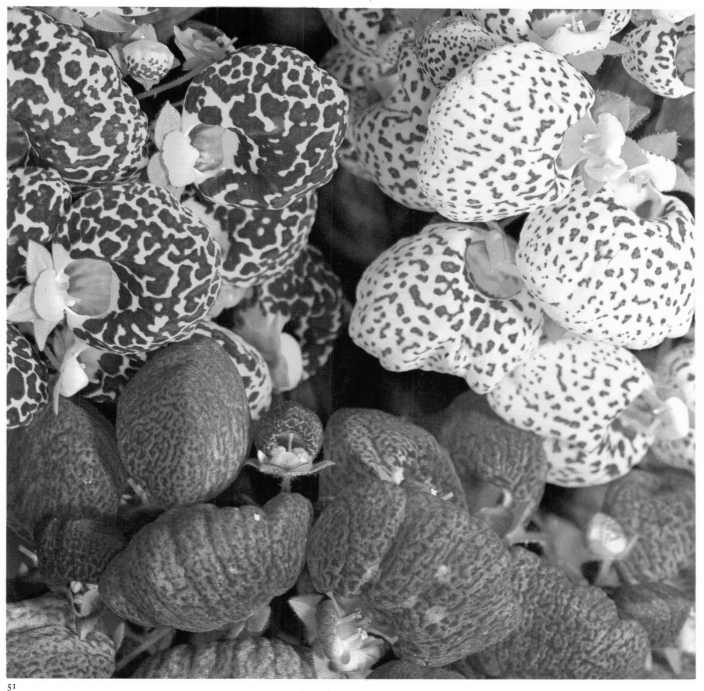

51

Callistemon

The callistemons, or Bottle-brush Trees, natives of Australia, have such unusual flowers (the numerous slender stamens in the form of a 'bottle-brush' constitute the 'flower') that they will appeal to many who have enough room to house them. *Callistemon citrinus* 'Splendens', with bright crimson stamens, is regarded as one of the finest in the genus and a mature tree will reach fifteen feet tall or more. *C. salignus* grows even taller and has yellow stamens, while *C. rigidus* 'Violaceus', up to eight feet, has purple stamens.

Callistemons are slow growers and can be pruned to keep them within bounds. They can be stood outside during the summer.

Camellia

One of the most beautiful plants suited to the house, that perfectly combines a savour of the exotic with the classical purity of its flowers. These range in size from small to two inches or more across; they may be single or double and the colours white, pink or rose to deep red or carmine. Camellias will flower in autumn, winter or spring and their dark, glossy, evergreen leaves are also attractive. They have the added advantage – for those with more space outside than in – that they prefer to be out of doors during the summer when they are not flowering.

There are numerous species, of which the most usually found are *Camellia japonica* (the Common Camellia), *C. reticulata* and *C. sasanqua*, and the richness of the genus has been greatly extended by the development of a wonderful range of cultivars of these species, extending from magnificent large blooms (some with combinations of colours) to exquisitely simple flowers like the single pure white 'Charlotte Rothschild' or single soft pink 'Elizabeth Rothschild'. *C. japonica* 'Adolphe Audusson', with large, semi-double, blood-red flowers in profusion, is one of the most dependable. *C.* × *williamsii* 'Donation', with soft pink semi-double flowers, has been called 'perhaps the most beautiful camellia raised this century'.* *C. sinensis*, the Tea Plant, which has leathery leaves and white flowers, has the distinction of being the only scented species.**

Camellias are not difficult to keep from year to year and will flower abundantly provided that a few elementary rules are obeyed. The plants must neither be over- nor under-watered and particular care must therefore be given to providing them with soil that is porous enough. They are acid-loving and should be fed periodically with sequestrene (iron chelate) or some other special camellia formula. Elbert and Hyams advise feeding them immediately after flowering with ammonium sulphate diluted one teaspoon to the gallon of water.

Some people find that camellia buds are susceptible to blast at the last moment and, again, Elbert and Hyams recommend uncapping the growth bud at the base of the flowering bud and using an eye-dropper to treat the opening with gibberellic acid. But as long as the plants are not allowed to become too dry they should flower easily enough.

Camellias are in general resistant to pests and diseases but they may be attacked by scale insects.

Cuttings, which will root much more easily if given bottom heat, may take up to three months to become established. They should be taken from nearly ripe wood towards the end of the growing season.

* *Hillier's Manual of Trees and Shrubs*, 1972, p. 62.

** Haskins Nurseries of Ferndown, Dorset, England specialize in some lovely cultivars of this species.

Campanula

Campanula is a large genus of which many species are hardy and can without difficulty be grown outside; these therefore do not concern us. There are a few species however that need protection from the cold and are worth cultivating as house or conservatory plants because they are attractive and easy to grow. Of these *Campanula isophylla* is perhaps the most useful because it has a trailing habit and can either be used in a basket or be allowed to hang down the side of a table or from a stand. The flowers are a clear lilac-blue but there is also a white variety, *C. isophylla alba*, much less attractive in our view. The only disadvantage of *C. isophylla* is that it dies back in the winter when it must be kept almost wholly dry. As soon as new growth starts to appear it should be encouraged with watering and some feeding.

C. pyramidalis is very different, putting forth tall, elongated spires of blue, bell-shaped flowers in the summer. It is a biennial and almost hardy.

52. *Callistemon citrinus splendens*

53. *Camellia japonica* 'Alba Simplex'

54. *Camellia × williamsii* 'St Ewe'

55. *Campanula isophylla*

52

53

54

55

Capsicum

Some people may like to vary their display of flowers and foliage with plants such as *Capsicum* and *Solanum* whose chief virtue in this context is their brightly coloured fruit or berries which ripen from green through yellow, orange and red to a deep purple-black. The small white or violet flowers have little attraction. Capsicums have an additional interest in that their fruits are the red pepper and the chilli that are used widely in cookery as vegetables or in the case of chillies as seasoning or dried and ground into Cayenne pepper.

Capsicum annuum, which produces the small red chillies, is the most usual species. It is an annual.

Capsicums usually appear in shops at an advanced stage of their cycle – with some fruit already ripe, but they can be raised from seed if you have the facilities. Seed should be sown in heat in February or March in boxes and thinned out as early as possible. Then, as soon as they can be handled easily, the seedlings should be transferred to 3-inch pots and later to 6- or 7-inch pots. The plants should be given plenty of sun to ensure that the fruit ripens.

They are prone to attack by white fly, red spider mite and begonia mite.

Caraguata – see GUZMANIA

Carex

The sedges are a very large genus of grass-like herbs, but mostly without enough distinction to be of much interest here. *Carex morrowii variegata*, as the name implies, is variegated, with a white line near each margin of its stiff,

pointed leaves and is evergreen. It adds variety to a group of foliage plants. In many catalogues this plant is found under its old name of *C. japonica*.

Carissa

Tough, spiny, shiny-leaved, evergreen shrubs that are admired even if they do not produce their fragrant white flowers and red or black berries, but if they do they are very rewarding and for this must have good summer sunlight.

Carissa grandiflora (the Natal Plum) is the best known species. *C. bispinosa*, unlike the others, does not need tropical or sub-tropical conditions.

Cassia

Some of the shrubs or small trees in this genus make attractive house plants when young but they soon tend to take up a lot of room.

The flowers of most species are yellow. The foliage is attractive. *Cassia auricularis* and, better, *C. corymbosa*, both with yellow

flowers, can be recommended. *C. fistula*, the Indian Laburnum, is a delightful tree with long, drooping racemes of yellow, fragrant flowers but in general grows too large to be practical. Another member of the family, *C. senna* provides the laxative senna.

Cattleya – see ORCHIDS

56. *Capsicum annuum*

57. *Carex morrowii variegata*

58. *Carissa grandiflora nana*

59. *Cassia corymbosa*

56

57

58

59

Centradenia

Useful, tough, evergreen shrubs with clusters of small rose-pink flowers. The late flowering season can last for several months. *Centradenia floribunda* and *C. grandifolia* are the best species.

Prune after flowering to keep a good shape.

Cereus – see CACTI

Ceropegia

Curious, semi-succulent plants with clusters of strangely shaped, tubular and usually small, white but purple-tinged, flowers. Best grown in a hanging basket. *Ceropegia woodii, C. elegans* or *C. rendallii* are perhaps the most attractive.

C. woodii has strings of heart-shaped leaves which are marbled green and silver on the upper side and are purple beneath; it forms corms on these strings and should be kept on the dry side.

Cestrum

Quite showy rambling shrubs, usually with pendulous sprays of numerous small tubular flowers. Those of *Cestrum aurantiacum* are orange and of *C. purpureum* reddish-purple; *C. × newellii*, which is of unconfirmed parentage, has bright crimson flowers. Although the greenish-yellow flowers of *C. nocturnum*, Night-blooming Jessamine, are not outstanding they have a delightful scent.

Whereas these shrubs flower in the summer if grown outside, they may be brought into flower in conservatories in late winter.

They can be pruned back quite hard after flowering.

Chamaecereus – see CACTI

Chamaedorea – see PALMS

Chamaerops – see PALMS

Cheiridopsis – see under MESEMBRYANTHEMUM

Chionodoxa – see BULBS

60

61

60. *Centradenia grandifolia*

61. *Ceropegia woodii*

62. *Cestrum aurantiacum*

62

Chlorophytum

Curious plants with long, grass-like, leaves and small white flowers on long stems, that can be grown in pots or hanging baskets. *Chlorophytum comosum* and its variety *variegatum*, whose leaves have a broad creamy-white central stripe, are viviparous – producing plantlets at the tips of the flower stems. *C. capense variegatum* has white edged leaves and is not viviparous.

Chorizema

Chorizema ilicifolium has a common name, the Holly Flame Pea, which is accurately descriptive, particularly in respect of the toothed leaves, but it is not a very satisfactory plant as it tends to produce weak straggly growth. *C. cordatum* is a much better bet, and even more so, its brilliant variety *splendens*. There are other species but *C. cordatum* is the only one that we have tracked down as available in the U.K. (Treseder). This, too, is straggly but can be ruthlessly cut back at any time.

Plants must not be allowed to become water-logged or they will quickly die.

Chrysanthemum

The forcing of chrysanthemums is one of the great specialized arts in gardening and is outside the scope of this book.

However chrysanthemums, usually dwarf varieties, are so widely offered as house plants that some notes on their care may be useful. The first task, as always, is to choose a healthy plant and, resisting the immediate impact of colour, one that has plenty of buds.

Then, in order to keep the plant in flower as long as possible it should be kept cool. 15° (59°F) is a very awkward daytime temperature for indoors but the more often or longer that a plant has to endure a higher temperature the shorter its flowering life will be. The plant should be watered frequently. Once it has flowered it is best thrown away unless you have a greenhouse.

Chrysanthemums are susceptible to a daunting array of diseases and pests but those bought direct from shops should be healthy and the only troubles that are likely are attacks of aphis or chrysanthemum miner; the latter is far away the most insidious but can be controlled by gamma-BHC, parathion or diazinon; malathion or a systemic insecticide without the ingredients named in the table on page 11 are also effective. If by chance there are signs of ill-health or the activity of pests the infected leaves should be removed and thrown away. Some insecticides contain chemicals that harm chrysanthemums and so before using a particular insecticide on them read the instructions carefully in case there is a warning against its use.

Cineraria – see under SENECIO

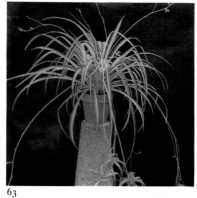

63

63. *Chlorophytum comosum variegatum*

64. *Chorizema ilicifolium*

65. *Chrysanthemum* 'Harmony'

66. *Chrysanthemum* 'Portrait'

67. *Chrysanthemum* 'Peggy Stevens'

64

65

66

67

Cissus

(C. antarctica)

The species are admired for their vine-like foliage rather than for their insignificant yellowish-green flowers and (usually) purple berries. The plants can be used as climbers or in hanging baskets.

Cissus adenopodus with green, red backed leaves and *C. discolor*, with purple silver and green marbled leaves, crimson backed, are the most resplendent species – but they can only be grown

successfully if you can create an atmosphere of tropical heat and moisture. *C. antarctica*, the Australian Kangaroo Vine, with handsome dark green leaves, will stand cool temperatures and not much light very well; it is therefore perhaps the most practical. Certainly its abundant foliage and rapid growth provide a delightful decoration against a blank, preferably white, wall.

Citrus

The genus *Citrus* offers the greatest reward of all to those house plant enthusiasts who love a combination of ornamental beauty and fragrance. Citruses have more to offer in flower and fruit for a longer period than perhaps any other plant that can be grown indoors. There is not long during the year when the elegant leaves are not accompanied by intoxicatingly scented flowers or decorative orange or yellow fruit.

The main snag is that citruses have the rather difficult requirement of a bright, moist but airy atmosphere or they will not prosper. Another snag is that some of them need rather a lot of space, but there are several species of lemon and lime that will flower and fruit when quite small.

Other species are *C. aurantifolia*, the acid lime, and *C. limetta*, the sweet or Persian lime; *C. limon*, lemon, and its variety *C. ponderosa*, also *C. × meyerii*, Meyer's Lemon, with lovely scented purple-tinged flowers; *C. paradisi*, grapefruit; *C. sinensis*, sweet orange; *C. ichangense*, the Ichang Lemon, and *C. taitensis*, the Otaheite dwarf orange. Then there is the *Citrus mitis* or Calamondin orange which is a native of the

Philippines, an enchanting miniature orange that bears tiny tangerine-shaped oranges and has delicately scented white flowers almost throughout the year.

Plants will benefit from being stood outside during the summer so that the wood can ripen but care should be taken not to transfer them suddenly from outside to a dry, centrally heated atmosphere or they will shed leaves and some of the branches will wither. If, however, this should happen, persevere: prune back carefully the dead wood and look after the plant until spring when new foliage will sprout.

Citruses are particularly prone to scale insects – and to red spider mite, which gets to work on the underside of the leaves causing them to yellow and drop: they must be watched very carefully to ensure that they remain healthy.

Propagation is difficult but worth trying: cuttings require a warm greenhouse or propagating frame and plants raised from pips, though easier, take four to six years before flowering and fruiting.

Clerodendrum

(Some species)

Only marginally suitable as house plants because they cannot be induced to flower unless they have a lot of light and a temperature of over 20° (68°F); also the climbing species are rampant. However they can be drastically pruned – which will encourage flowering – and can also be adapted to hanging baskets. The striking clusters of flowers that appear in profusion on those plants offered for sale tempt one to try one's luck; and they make magnificent conservatory plants.

There are two main categories of clerodendrum: the climbing and the shrubby. Of the first, *Clerodendrum thomsonae* is the most noteworthy. At its best it will throw forth gorgeous cascades of white, heart-shaped calyces (sepals) from which

project startling deep red corollas with prominent stamens. The white calyx gradually darkens to pink. In ideal conditions this species will flower almost continuously but most people will be thankful for one flowering season, in early summer.

Of the shrubby species *C. speciosissimum* is the most likely to be offered for sale. The panicles of bright scarlet flowers appear – again under ideal conditions – in profusion. This species, unlike *C. thomsonae*, unfortunately sheds its large leaves in winter. *C. fragrans* is also deciduous but its pinkish-white flowers are, as the name denotes, scented.

During the period of growth the plants need a lot of water.

68. *Cissus antarctica*

69. *Citrus calamondia*

70. *Citrus persea*

71. *Clerodendrum speciosissimum*

72. *Clerodendrum thomsonae*

69

70

71

72

Clianthus

Sturt's Desert Pea or the Glory Pea, *Clianthus formosus* is a native of Australia and has strikingly flamboyant brilliant red flowers with a purplish black base. It has a creeping habit and so makes a delightful plant for a hanging basket from which its branches can trail down. The soil should always be very well drained. In order to obtain longer-lasting, more reliable plants seedlings are commonly grafted onto seedlings of *Colutea arborescens*.

Plants are prone to red spider mite.

Clivia

An impressive member of the amaryllis family, comprising three species of which *Clivia miniata* with its bright orange-red to yellow flowers is the most popular. Clivias are unusual among the amaryllids in having evergreen foliage. *C. miniata* also has attractive red berry-like fruits.

Clivias are very tough and should be treated like hippeastrums (q.v.), except that they seldom need re-potting.

Coccoloba

The only species in this large genus that is of interest in this context is *Coccoloba uvifera*, the Seaside Grape. In its natural state it will grow to some twenty feet and will produce racemes of fragrant white flowers, then purplish 'berries' spotted with green.

As a house plant it will grow to little more than three feet and is unlikely to flower but its large, glossy, almost round, wavy leaves are attractive.

Cocos – see PALMS, under *Syagrus*

Codiaeum

The best that can be said of codiaeums is that they bring an element of the tropics into the house. Their rather garish, stiff, prominently veined leaves of varying shades of green, yellow and reddish brown do give a striking effect of contrast to a group of milder foliage plants.

The shoots may be selectively stopped to produce bushy plants or they can be allowed to be single-stemmed.

If codiaeums are subjected to cold or if there are too violent changes in temperature they are apt to shed their leaves.

They are prone to red spider unless the atmosphere is moist enough, also to thrips.

Codiaeums are sometimes mistakenly called crotons. The plants most usually grown are forms of *Codiaeum variegatum pictum* and vary both in the shape and colour of leaf.

Coelogyne – see ORCHIDS

73. *Clianthus formosus*

74. *Clivia miniata*

75. *Coccoloba uvifera*

76. *Codiaeum* 'Volcano'

73

74

75

76

Coffea

Coffea arabica is the species that is used for the production of Arabian coffee 'beans'. It has glossy dark green leaves and when small makes an attractive foliage plant. If you have enough space you can allow the plant to develop further when it will produce clusters of fragrant white flowers followed by berries (from which the beans are extracted) that ripen to red.

Plants may be pruned quite drastically. Other species are unlikely to be available. *C. arabica* likes plenty of air and humidity.

Cuttings should be taken from mature growth.

Coleus

A genus of some 150 species from the tropics in the Old World. *Coleus blumei* and its varieties, the commonest species, is really better as a bedding than as a house plant because the extraordinary variegations of colour on the leaves – yellow, pink, red, copper, crimson, sometimes combined with green, and so on – appear more effective when the plants are grouped and contrasted together.

But there are people who have a passion for coleus and are able to make enough space for an impressive show indoors or else will group them attractively with other foliage plants.

One is advised, rightly, to pinch out the buds of the insigni-

ficant flowers except in the case of *C. frederici*, *C. thyrsoideus* and a few other species which have tall panicles of bright blue or purple flowers, scented in the former, with the great advantage of appearing in the winter.

Most *C. blumei* are best kept for one season only but cuttings root very easily at all times of the year. As the plant matures the tips should be pinched out to give bushiness and shape.

Coleus plants are very prone to mealy bug and green fly, etc. They may also be attacked by leaf eelworm for which thionazin or parathion are currently the best remedies.

Collinia – see PALMS

Columnea

This genus of evergreen plants from tropical South America is closely related to the Malaysian *Aeschynanthus*; it has a number of pendulous species that make attractive basket plants. Among them are *Columnea gloriosa* with fiery-red tubular flowers, yellow in the throat (the variety *purpurea* has purple leaves when young, turning to bronze); *C. oerstediana*

(russet orange flowers); and *C. rotundifolia* with large, long crimson flowers, often in winter.

For cultivation, see *Aeschynanthus*. Like *Aeschynanthus* columnea must have a high degree of humidity or their leaves and buds will drop.

Commelina

Closely related to tradescantias with small, usually deep blue flowers. These are short-lived (hence the common name, Day

Flower) but they appear in profusion. Some species have variegated leaves. Easily grown.

Conophytum – see under MESEMBRYANTHEMUM

58

77. *Coffea arabica*

78. *Coleus blumei* 'Salmon Lace'

79. *Columnea gloriosa purpurea*

80. *Commelina tuberosa*

77

78

79

80

Convallaria

bulb fibre

The solitary species in this genus, *Convallaria majalis*, the Lily of the Valley, is of course grown outdoors with ease in a temperate climate. It has, however, been included here on the same principle as a number of bulbs; that is to say that it can be brought into flower during the winter if given enough warmth, which its delicate purity and fragrance makes well worthwhile.

Lilies of the Valley are supplied in the form of 'crowns' or 'pips' which consist of buds with roots, cut off from the root stock. These should be placed close together in peat potting fibre with a charcoal base, the tops just showing above the surface, which can be covered with a layer of moss to help preserve the moisture and as decoration.

If the crowns have been treated for forcing – i.e. kept at a temperature just below freezing point for three months – flowers will appear about a month after planting provided only that they are given a temperature of around 20° (68°F) during the day. If the crowns have not been so treated they will need bottom heat between 20° and 25° (about 75°F) to bring them quickly into flower.

The fibre – or whatever medium is used – must always be kept moist and when the flower buds appear they should be given plenty of light but must be protected from direct sun.

It should be emphasised that only crowns with plump, healthy buds should be chosen.

Convolvulus

Among this genus of predominantly trailing or climbing species there is one at least that is well worth the attention of house plant cultivators. This is *Convolvulus cneorum*, a graceful, compact shrub with thin leaves covered with soft, silvery hairs; the flowers, like larger versions of *C. arvensis*, the common bindweed, come singly at the ends of the shoots.

Plants are undemanding and relatively trouble-free. They should not be kept in an atmosphere with high humidity and a high temperature or the flower may yellow and wither.

C. cneorum is almost hardy and so can be stood outside during the summer.

Cordyline

One of the most elegant foliage plants – although in their native habitat cordylines will also have panicles of usually small, creamy, scented flowers.

The long pointed leaves of the varieties of *Cordyline terminalis* can have the most brilliant combinations of colour, usually of green and bright pink or red. Cordylines tend to be expensive because the colouring does not develop fully until the plants are several seasons old.

The plants are relatively immune to pests except red spider mite.

Cordylines are often confused with dracaenas, q.v.

Propagation from existing stock is somewhat impractical since it must be by a stem cutting which mutilates the parent plant.

Correa

These shrubs with their numerous tubular flowers have a quiet appeal; what is more they flower during the winter and for a long season.

Correa pulchella has pale red or vermilion flowers, *C. reflexa*

(syns. *C. rubra, C. speciosa*), in Australia called Native Fuchsia – has rich red flowers tipped with yellow or green; *C. × mannii* is a lovely hybrid of these two, with deep red flowers. *C. × harrisii* makes an attractive bush, with yellowish-green flowers.

81

82

83

84

Coryphantha – see CACTI

Cotyledon

Most of the species once classified under *Cotyledon* have been transferred to other genera, preponderantly to *Echeveria*. Of what is left the shrubby evergreen, rather than deciduous, plants are of interest here. All cotyledons are succulent.

Cotyledon undulata is perhaps the best species. Its leaves have wavy edges and are covered with a white meal. The red,

tubular flowers are often pendent. Plants of this species should not have their leaves wettened or they will lose the white bloom. *C. coccinea* is now known as *Rochea coccinea* (q.v.).

Plants may be attacked by aphides at the inflorescence.

Crassula

The name-giver of the family Crassulaceae. A large genus of succulent herbs and shrubs of very varied form and texture, mostly from South Africa.

Elbert and Hyams, with good reason, strongly recommend *Crassula portulacea* – popularly called the Jade Plant – for its 'sculptural', 'Chinese look' and because the plants 'grow into superb specimens with thick trunks which make them look very ancient and noble'.

Another, very different species is *C. sarcocaulis* which is a shrubby little plant with a mass of small pink flowers. It is hardy enough to grow in a rock garden but will make quite an attractive addition to a grouping of succulents.

C. coccinea is a synonym of *Rochea coccinea* (q.v.).

Crocus – see BULBS

Crossandra

A small genus of attractive little plants that are quite widely offered for sale during the summer. They bear their primrose-like flowers on terminal spikes. The flowers may be pale lilac

in the case of *Crossandra guineensis* or orange in *C. smithii* or red-orange in *C. nilotica* or *C. infundibuliformis* (syn. *C. undulifolia*).

Croton – see CODIAEUM

85, 86. *Cotyledon undulata*

87. *Crassula arborescens*

88. *Crossandra smithii*

85

86

87

88

Cryptanthus

Unlike most bromeliads cryptanthus do not have very interesting flowers but they are valued chiefly for the brightly coloured or curiously patterned foliage of some species and varieties. The more soberly coloured species are of little interest.

The most spectacular is *Cryptanthus bromelioides tricolor* whose long, pointed leaves are striped with pink, yellow, creamy-white and green: as if the plant had been decorated for a carnival. Other striking species are the small *C. bivittatus* with toothed slightly wavy leaves that have two buff stripes; the variety *roseo-pictus* has pink stripes as the name denotes.

Then there are *C. fosterianus*, the largest, with stripes of various colours running *across* the leaves, rather similar to *C. zonatus*; and *C. acaulis*, of which the variety *rubra* makes a striking plant when the white flowers are out against the background of mauvish leaves.

The usual guide-lines for bromeliads (see *Aechmea*) apply except that cryptanthus are terrestrial yet with a rather slight root system and some of them do not have the usual vase: thus keeping the right degree of moisture is a problem. They should be moist in summer, on the dry side in winter.

Ctenanthe – see under MARANTA

Cyanotis

A rather undistinguished genus closely related to *Tradescantia*, although tending to be more compact in habit. It is perhaps best used as part of a grouping of foliage plants although it will

in fact produce panicles of tiny blue flowers in the case of *Cyanotis barbata* and some other species, or rose in the case of *C. kewensis*.

Cyclamen

The cyclamen is probably the most consistently popular of all flowering pot plants which is a tribute to its grace and other qualities because, in fact, it epitomises the problems that face any lover of plants in the house. Cyclamen flower in the winter and like, indeed demand, conditions that are diametrically opposed to those that prevail at this season in even the most civilised of houses. They need light, a constant, cool temperature around 15° (59°F) and a high degree of moisture in the atmosphere; they do not like draughts. Thus it is not surprising that there are many disconcertingly quick casualties among even the most resplendent plants, with the leaves yellowing and the buds wilting.

Great care must be taken with watering as the plant must neither get too dry nor too wet. Rochford and Gorer advise keeping the pot plunged in damp peat which is an excellent safeguard because then very little actual watering of the plant is necessary. But don't forget to keep the peat moist.

Whether you water from the top or by immersing the pot in water depends on how the plant has been grown. If the crown of the corm is above the surface of the soil you can water in the ordinary way from the top without doing harm. If, on the other hand, the corm is fully buried it is wiser to water by immersing the pot in water three-quarters up for a few

minutes. The danger to avoid is allowing rot to set in at the top of the corm where the leaves and buds sprout. However if you use the second method do not let the pot become water-logged. It must again be emphasised that the only hope of keeping cyclamen in good health is to have the soil rather dry, but the atmosphere as moist as possible and to provide plenty of light.

After the plant has flowered the leaves will continue to grow for some six to eight weeks and so you should continue to tend it with water. The longer that it grows at this stage the better it will be next year. When the leaves begin to yellow stop watering and allow the plant to dry out, then store it in a dry, dark place.

In July bring the pot back to a light place and start watering – very gently at first until there are clear signs of growth. (If it has been in a 3½-inch pot it is best to transfer it to a 5-inch one.) As growth begins, start to fertilize regularly. With care the plant will flower again in December or January. Three seasons are about as long as the plants stay at their best.

When you first buy a cyclamen make sure that it is a really healthy plant with strong dark foliage. It is best for the plant

89

90

91

89. *Cryptanthus fosterianus*

90. *Cyanotis kewensis*

91. *Cyclamen persicum*
(wild form)

to have a few flowers open and plenty of well-advanced buds. The change of atmosphere from nursery to shop and from shop to home will inevitably have been harmful and some of the smaller buds may well not develop. So at least ensure that you get your money's worth with a good month's flowering in the first season.

Many will agree that the original, wild *Cyclamen persicum* that grows in Greece and Asia Minor, with its marbled leaves and delicately graceful, small, fragrant flowers on long stems is more beautiful than the coarser, more flamboyant cultivated varieties but if you do not have the good fortune to have seen the wild cyclamen you may not pine for it and should be happy with the handsome and by no means ungraceful cultivated cyclamen.* The 'silver leaf' strain is admired also for its foliage.

Provided that you can keep the soil and the atmosphere at the right level of moisture cyclamen are not particularly prone to disease. If there is too much moisture the plant may be attacked by fungus disease and should be treated with a copper lime dust. Too dry an atmosphere, on the other hand, will make the plant prone to red spider mite. When any leaves turn yellow remove them carefully at the base so that they do not set up rot.

Although not common in well-tended plants tarsonemid mites may attack plants. This is revealed by rust-coloured patches on the younger leaves and causes distortion of leaves and stunting of growth. They can be countered by dicofol, endrin or endosulfan. Vine weevils and leaf miner may also appear; gamma-BHC and thionazin are the best remedies.

* A dwarf, small-flowered strain that is scented has recently been developed.

Cymbidium – see ORCHIDS

Cyperus

Some species in this genus of rush- or grass-like herbs make graceful house plants. *Cyperus alternifolius* with umbrella-ribs of leaves at the end of one- to two-foot stems is particularly recommended. *C. diffusus*, a larger plant, is also attractive, particularly in a group of various plants; on a grander scale, in a conservatory for instance, it makes a fine water plant.

Cyperus cannot have too much water and is best left standing in a dish of water. It also has the advantage of not requiring much light. Its only drawback is a tendency for the tips of the leaves to turn brown from draughts – or too little water.

Cypripedium – see ORCHIDS, under *Paphiopedilum*

Cyrtomium – see FERNS

Cytisus

Cytisus, together with the closely related *Genista* and *Spartium*, is commonly grouped under the general heading of 'broom'. Most brooms are hardy enough to grow satisfactorily outdoors but among the more tender species, *Cytisus canariensis*, the 'Genista' of florists, a compact bush with abundant, faintly fragrant yellow flowers in the spring (or earlier if a temperature of 20° (68°F) can be provided) is a delightful house plant. *C. supranubius* (Teneriffe Broom, syns. *Genista fragrans*, *Spartocytisus nubigenus*), although considerably larger has fragrant white flowers touched with pink and is also worth having indoors.

When the danger of frost has gone plants will benefit by being stood outside in a sunny position but they must on no account be neglected as they need plenty of water during the summer and also periodic feeding. As much care should be taken to avoid over-watering when the plants are indoors as to avoid under-watering in the summer, because they are easily damaged and may drop their buds.

After flowering the young shoots of the plant may be trimmed back.

92. *Cyperus diffusus*

93. *Cytisus supranubius*

94. *Damnacanthus indicus*

95. *Datura suaveolens*

92

93

94

95

Damnacanthus

Dainty evergreen shrubs with layers of thin, closely packed, spiny branches and small, shiny, heart-shaped leaves. The two most usually found species, *Damnacanthus indicus* and *D. major* bear masses of small white flowers that in the case of *D. major* are fragrant, and brilliant scarlet little berries.

Their compact growth and ornamental appearance make them most attractive house plants which when still small resemble Bonsai trees; they deserve to be more widely known.

Datura

The finest species in this genus have such exotically beautiful and fragrant trumpet-shaped flowers that they deserve inclusion despite the fact that some are annuals whereas others tend to be large and leggy; the latter can in fact be pruned ruthlessly. Some species have important medicinal qualities but others may be highly poisonous.

Among the best perennial species are *Datura arborea* (Angel's Trumpet), with enormous yellowish-white flowers; *D. cornigera* or *knightii*, with creamy white flowers (usually double in *D. knightii*), very fragrant at night; *D. meteloides* with breathtaking large pale violet or, in some varieties, rose or white tinted fragrant flowers; and *D. suaveolens* with white fragrant flowers.

Plants should be given plenty of fertilizer and water during the growing season but be kept on the dry side in the winter; they can be stood outside during the summer. A close watch should be kept for red spider mite.

Cuttings root very easily over bottom heat.

Davallia – see FERNS

Dendrobium – see ORCHIDS

Dendromecon

An attractive, striking shrub, *Dendromecon rigidum* has handsome, slender pointed leaves on bamboo-coloured wood and single, yellow flowers like large buttercups, with a deliciously fresh scent of cucumber.* This plant may flower as early as February. *D. harfordii* has ovate leaves and considerably larger yellow flowers; its variety *rhamnoides* has similar but blue-green leaves and paler yellow flowers.

Plants are apt to get a bit leggy but can safely be pruned back after flowering.

It is however a difficult plant because it must have very good drainage and a dry atmosphere but will quickly die if allowed to dry out. Also the plants dislike having their roots disturbed. We have had more casualties with this plant than with any other.

* We owe the identification of the scent to Messrs Treseder.

Desfontainea

Desfontainea spinosa is a plant that deserves to be more widely known than it is. It has evergreen holly-like leaves and produces numerous flame-coloured tubular flowers with yellow tips, usually in late summer.

Plants need to be particularly well drained and the soil should be free of lime. Propagation by seed is more reliable than by cuttings.

Dichorisandra

Dichorisandra mosaica is an attractive plant which will put forth a head of bright blue flowers from a sheath of striking leaves: purplish beneath and dark green above, spattered with fine horizontal white lines. Its variety *undata* is smaller and much more compact with alternate, silvery- and blackish-green vertical stripes on its larger, wavy leaves. *D. reginae*

also has curiously patterned leaves: green shading to white, often tinged with purple along the midrib and purple beneath. Its flowers are white tinged with blue.

Plants should be protected from direct sun in the summer.

Dictyosperma – see PALMS

96

98

96. *Dendromecon rigidum*

97. *Desfontainea spinosa*

98. *Dichorisandra reginae*
(left), *Pellionia repens*
(right)

97

Dieffenbachia

In natural conditions dieffenbachias grow to six feet and more but when young they make quite an elegant contribution to a grouping of foliage plants although we do not particularly recommend them in isolation. The leaves are usually large, green and mottled with cream or white. *D. amoena*, *D. arvida* 'Exotica' (very variegated) and the varieties of *D. picta* are those most often found.

Unfortunately dieffenbachias are among the more tender foliage plants and need as close a reproduction of the warm, humid atmosphere of the rainy tropics as is possible. The minimum winter temperature should not fall below 15° (59°F) or 20° (68°F) in the case of *D. picta* and its varieties.

The sap of dieffenbachias is poisonous.

Cuttings will root quite well with bottom heat, or the suckers thrown up by the plants can be detached and potted separately, or pieces of stem, one to two inches long, can be slightly dried and then rooted in a propagating frame.

Dipladenia

Very attractive evergreen climbing plants that should be much more widely known.

Dipladenia splendens, with pale pink trumpet-shaped flowers is the species most usually found but there are also other delightful species, hybrids and varieties.

Dipladenias should flower continuously throughout the summer. When flowering is over the new growth should be selectively pruned back; once the plant has reached the size that is wanted all new growth should be pruned back. In fact plants can be turned into bushes rather than climbers if this is wanted.

Dipladenias are naturally evergreen but may shed their leaves indoors if the atmosphere becomes too dry. They like a high degree of moisture and humidity during their active period but the soil must be well drained or the leaves will quickly yellow and drop. They are very prone to attacks by aphides and red spider mite.

Cuttings from young shoots, or from pieces of stem with two leaves and about an inch below, root easily with high bottom heat, from 25–30° (77–86°F).

Dizygotheca

Dizygotheca elegantissima, the member of this small genus that is generally on offer, has a particularly graceful spread of slender toothed, brownish-mauve leaves flecked with white and makes an ideal foil to other, broad leaved foliage plants or shrubs.

Unfortunately it is very tender, likes a lot of moisture (or it will succumb to red spider mite) and prefers the temperature not to go below 15° (59°F). It is a very slow grower.

D. elegantissima used to be known as *Aralia elegantissima*.

99

100

101

Dracaena

A larger more varied genus than *Cordyline* with which it is frequently confused. *Dracaena deremensis* is like a cordyline with silver striped leaves. *D. fragrans* 'Massangeana' is a tree-like plant with long, pointed leaves and, in its native habitat, clustered yellow scented flowers. It will grow very tall but usually has its head cut off when about three to four feet high; this induces sprouts of leaves from various points and although one might expect the result to look ungainly it is in fact impressive. *D. marginata* is very elegant with soft, light grey bark and similarly shaped dark green leaves margined with red. *D. sanderiana* is a several branched plant with greyish green leaves shot with ivory.

Like cordylines, young dracaenas need a lot of light, heat and moisture to bring them to their full colouring but once the plant is mature it is less exacting. Each of the species mentioned should, however, be kept on the dry side in winter except for *D. marginata* that needs rather more moisture to prevent the tips of the leaves from browning. Do not spray either genus when the atmosphere is cool because water lodging in the leaf joints can do harm.

Drejerella *guttata* – see BELOPERONE

Duranta

Duranta repens is a most attractive shrub with a mass of small blue, purple, or white flowers and yellow berries on, usually pendent, sprays. It is well worth getting hold of if possible. *D. plumieri* is apparently a synonym.

Plants need the standard treatment for shrubs from the rainy tropics. They are very fast growing but can be trimmed without harm.

Green fly seem to have an obsessive attachment to the young shoots and white fly to the leaves.

Echeveria

Perhaps the most exciting of the family Crassulaceae to which the *Kalanchoe* and *Sedum* also belong. The leaves are in rosettes but vary a lot in shape and colour.

Echeveria retusa hybrida has red margins to its glaucous green leaves and plenty of crimson-pink flowers in the winter. *E. gibbiflora* has a purplish tinge to its waxy grey-blue leaves and scarlet flowers in the summer. *E. harmsii* (also known as *Coty-*

ledon elegans, *Oliveranthus elegans* and *Echeveria elegans*) is a branching plant with relatively large, inch-long tubular, red flowers, opening outwards at the ends and yellow inside.

The plants should be shaded from strong sun but be given plenty of light. Do not over-water or they will become rampant and lose their attractive symmetry.

Echinopsis – see CACTI

Elentheropetalum *ernestii-augustii* – see PALMS under *Chamaedorea*

102

103

104

105

106

107

Elettaria

A member of the Zingiberaceae or ginger family, *Elettaria cardamomum* is the illustrious source of cardamom seeds, the 'Seeds of Paradise' which feature so widely in oriental cookery and indeed life, being also chewed as a breath freshener with the (claimed) qualities of acting as a stimulant, a carminative and an antiseptic.* Alas the flowers and therefore the fruit are none too easy to induce** but the foliage is graceful; moreover the leaves will impart a delightful lemony scent to your hand if you brush it gently through them. In its natural habitat the plant's many stems will grow up to ten feet high but as a pot plant you are unlikely to find it much taller than two feet.

It is a rather exacting plant and needs good light but shading from direct sun as well as plenty of a fully balanced nutrient if it is to give of its very worthwhile best.

Elettaria cardamomum is sometimes – wrongly – called *Amomum cardamomum*.

* The curious will find an authoritative exposition of the plant and its qualities (together with an excellent illustration) in Grieve, *A Modern English Herbal*, 1931, under the entry Cardamoms.
** We may be being pessimistic here because there seems to be no particular reason why this should be so. It is just that our plants have *not* yet produced flowers or fruit. The rhizomes and stems proliferate fast and it may be best to do some ruthless thinning out to encourage strong growth.

Epacris

    peat and silver sand

This, chiefly Australian, genus is rather similar in appearance and requirements to the Cape heaths (*Erica*, q.v.) but has the advantage of more striking flowers and of being somewhat easier to acclimatise to indoor conditions.

Most species are erect but a few are pendent and these are perhaps the most attractive. *Epacris longiflora*, with long as its

name denotes, tubular flowers, crimson but white at the ends, has a long flowering season. *E. obtusifolia* is erect but has delightfully scented small creamy-white flowers.

Like heaths *Epacris* need very careful watering, lime-free soil, and must not be allowed to dry out. Also like heaths, they are best kept outside during the summer.

Epiphyllum – see CACTI

Episcia

Episcias have striking foliage as well as quite attractive flowers and a very long flowering season. Some species such as *Episcia cupreata*, *E. fulgida* and *E. lilacina* (the first scarlet, the second with vermilion and the third with pale bluish-lilac or lavender flowers) have a creeping habit and so are good for a hanging

basket. Several named cultivars have been introduced into the U.S.A.

If the plants are kept in pots particular care must be paid to the drainage.

Eranthemum

A small genus of shrubs; most plants referred to as *Eranthemum* belonging in fact to the genus *Pseuderanthemum*.

Eranthemum pulchellum is a nice plant to have because it will produce clusters of small dark blue flowers in the winter.

Plants should be cut back after flowering so that they do not become leggy and they may need potting on.

They are prone to attack by scale insects.

Erica

    peat and silver sand

If heaths did not flower in the winter and were not so widely offered and bought we should not have included them here because they may not even survive successfully the jolt of transfer from a shop to a house and are in general difficult to keep in good condition indoors.

Those species with which we are concerned are the Cape heaths from South Africa. *Erica hyemalis* with white tubular flowers tinged with pink is one of the most outstanding species. *E. gracilis* has smaller but abundant rose coloured or, in a variety, white flowers and *E. pageana* has yellow flowers.

Ericas need a light situation free from draughts, well away from the hot air or fumes given off by any source of heat. In

fact they will do best if kept at a temperature below 20° (68°F). They must also have plenty of moisture but good drainage. If the soil is allowed to become dry the plants will drop their leaves and flowers and may well not recover. Thus if they are supplied in small pots it is wise to re-pot them immediately: the roots are easy to handle and the plant should not suffer. They must have an acid soil.

Many people will feel that they have done well to have successfully completed one flowering season and will be tempted to call it a day. But in fact the worst should now be over and although constant attention is of course essential it should be possible to bring the plants through to further flowering

114. *Eucalyptus globulus*

115. *Eucalyptus citriodora*

116. *Eucharis grandiflora*

115

114

116

Eucharis

An outstandingly attractive member of the Amaryllidaceae with umbels of white, delightfully scented, slightly drooping, narcissus-like flowers on a stalk up to two feet long. *Eucharis grandiflora*, the Amazon Lily, is the best known species but there are others of equal beauty.

Bulbs should be planted in the spring in a temperature of about 20° (68°F) and, as with similar plants, they should not be fully covered with soil. They need a moist atmosphere and plenty of water when they are growing but good drainage. They should be protected from full summer sun. During the winter they should be kept only just moist enough to prevent the leaves from withering.

They will normally flower in the late spring or summer but can be induced into doing so earlier and will quite probably have a second season later on; they should then be stopped from any further flowering – by reducing nutrients and pinching out buds – until the following year because otherwise the bulbs may be weakened. Off-shoots can be separated from the main bulb (with care not to disturb its roots) and grown on their own.

They are prone to attack by pests such as mealy bug and red spider mite; as well as the eponymous eucharis mite.

Euphorbia

The genus *Euphorbia* is large and varied, ranging from globular cactus-like plants – *Euphorbia meloformis* – to trees up to forty feet high such as *E. tetragona*.

In this context, however, the genus is dominated by *E. pulcherrima*, the Poinsettia. The Poinsettia, with its spectacular brilliant red bracts, deserves its immense popularity, particularly at Christmas, as a decorative plant.

It is a tribute to the plant's splendour that growers have persevered so long with an apparently intractable subject. In fact it was only in 1964 with the introduction of the Mikkelsen strain that they were able to claim success in producing a tough, small, shapely plant that could withstand house conditions; and this has only been achieved with the aid of chemical dwarfing compounds.

It will almost certainly be the Mikkelsen strain that is offered in profusion around Christmas by the best growers and shops. Nonetheless plants can be very disappointing and quickly shed their leaves unless they are bought in the peak of condition and unless certain fundamental rules are observed.

Therefore be particularly careful in choosing your plant. It must look sturdy, with the leaves a rich green, without any sign of yellowing or wilting. Furthermore you will have a longer-lasting plant if the minute flowers at the centre of the bracts are not yet out or only just coming out. The flowers 'drop' once they are over and although this does not matter because they are so insignificant their dropping will in due course be followed by the shedding of the leaves and then the bracts. The interval can vary a lot but it is clearly best to get a plant at the start rather than the end of its flowering cycle.

Once you have the plant in a room you must see that it is not in a draughty position, that the temperature does not fall below 10° (50°F) and ideally stays at around 15° (59°F) or a little above and that the atmosphere is as moist as possible: put the pot on a bed of wet peat or of Stenetter pebbles and syringe it as often as possible when the temperature goes above 20° (68°F). Keep the soil in the pot itself moist, neither wet nor dry, with water at room temperature. (There is no need to bother particularly about light when the bracts are fully formed.) The closer that you can keep to these conditions the longer the plant will last – which can be well over a month, making it one of the most satisfying and cheap forms of flower decoration that you can buy.

When the leaves and bracts have finally been shed you must decide whether to be patiently ambitious or to call it a day. If the latter, throw the plant away; if the former, cut off the flower heads and keep the plant barely moist for the rest of the winter. In April cut it back to some four inches of stem and water more liberally. When shoots three to four inches long have sprouted you should take them as cuttings if you have a greenhouse and bring them on in a No. 1 soil mixture, transferring them to No. 3 when they have fully rooted. They should be given as much light as possible with the temperature at least 20° (68°F) during the day, but shaded from strong direct sun and they should be fed every three weeks. If you do not have the conditions for raising cuttings you should re-pot the old plant in a No. 1 soil mixture when you cut back in April, then transfer it to a No. 3 mixture after the plant has sprouted three- or four-inch shoots and follow the same instructions as for the rooted cuttings.

Whether you take cuttings or persevere with the old plant you should be able to produce flowers by Christmas or a few weeks later. However, without the help of chemical dwarfing compounds the plants will be somewhat leggy and you are unlikely to achieve such full bracts as are found on those for sale in the shops.

Poinsettias are prone to white fly and green fly; they must be watched carefully and treated with an aerosol if any appear.

Through some perversity growers are now offering a pink and a white variety of Poinsettia.

Of the other euphorbias, *E. fulgens*, Scarlet Plume, makes an attractive conservatory plant with its clusters of brilliant little scarlet-bracted flowers on long stems. It is however inclined to become leggy and needs more space than is usually available in a room. It should be given a No. 1 soil mix.

Then there are a group of succulents of which *E. milii*, Crown of Thorns (often called *E. splendens*), is frequently offered as a house plant. In nature it will grow to a vast straggling shrub and is used for hedges but indoors it is a fairly slow grower and, as it flowers when very young, it will make a curiously original house plant with small red-bracted flowers and sparse little leaves on dry-looking, brown thorny stems. It should be given a No. 2 mix with very good drainage. It needs plenty of water when in growth but very little when inactive. The flowering season can be quite long.

Euphorbia tirucalii, the Pencil Plant, is a striking succulent tree with masses of small tubular branches (hence its popular name), usually without leaves. The flowers are insignificant.

117. *Euphorbia fulgens*

118. *Euphorbia pulcherrima* (Mikkelsen strain)

117

118

Euryops

A genus of attractive evergreen shrubs with, usually, large, yellow daisy-like flowers. *Euryops abrotanifolius*, and some hybrids have the great advantage of flowering in the late winter.

Exacum

Exacum affine is a particularly delightful annual or biennial small bush – about a foot high – with a mass of sweetly scented little mauve flowers with yellow anthers.

Seed should be sown from February to May in a temperature of at least 15° (59°F) but preferably 20° (68°F) for late summer and autumn flowering. Seeds can also be sown in the late summer for flowering the following year. Larger and better plants will be got this way but the other is much easier.

x Fatshedera

This is a bi-generic hybrid formed by the crossing of *Hedera hibernica* with *Fatsia japonica* 'Moseri'. It is as easy a plant to keep healthy as common ivy and, though slow-growing, rather more attractive both in its ordinary and variegated form, hence its popularity.

For further details, see *Hedera*.

Fatsia

Fatsia japonica is a hardy evergreen shrub with large, palmate, shiny dark green leaves. It also has curious flowers like those of the ivy but much larger. There is a variegated form with white tipped leaves.

F. japonica used to be known as *Aralia japonica* or *A. sieboldii*.

Faucaria – see under MESEMBRYANTHEMUM

119. *Euryops acraeus* (syn. *E. evansii*)

120. *Exacum affine*

121. × *Fatshedera lizei*

122. *Fatsia japonica*

119

120

121

122

Ferns

Most ferns have a gentle, graceful appeal that may be overlooked but, once appreciated, they can exert a strong hold on the imagination.

There is a vast range of ferns. Some ten thousand different species grow from the tropics to the arctic circle; and within this area, as would be expected, there are ferns of the most varying habits and forms. Many, though not all, are moisture- and shade-loving; some are epiphytic; some thrive in high temperatures, some in low; some grow as high as fifty feet and some no more than a few inches; some, such as most of those in North America, are deciduous, others, such as most of the Japanese ferns, are evergreen.

With the great differences in habitat come similar differences in cultural requirements. There are those at one end of the scale that demand stove conditions and at the other those that are very hardy. Here we are concerned with the middle range which in fact provides plenty of variety, both in form and in the decorative use to which they can be put.

The genus *Adiantum* itself offers considerable variety, from the delicate, lacy-fronded *Adiantum capillus-veneris*, the Maidenhair Fern and kindred species, to the simpler, more luxuriant looking *A. macrophyllum*.* A disadvantage of this genus is that not all species are evergreen. *A. cuneatum* is very similar to *A. capillus-veneris*, and easier to grow; *A. tinctum* has even more delicate fronds which are a pretty rose colour when young. *A. macrophyllum* has larger fronds, up to fifteen inches tall, the strong, erect stems carrying pairs of oval to arrow-shaped green leaflets (striped and spotted white in the variety *albo-striata*); and *A. peruvianum** is another larger species. Then there are *A. pulverulentum*,* with feathery acacia-like fronds; and *A. caudatum* and *A. gracillimum*, both pendulous and well suited to hanging baskets.

Asplenium (Spleenwort) is also an attractive and wide-ranging genus, with the advantage of being evergreen and relatively easy to cultivate. *Asplenium attenuatum* has narrow, wavy fronds up to a foot long, tapering to a point at which curious crests – small plantlets shaped like the flowers of a *Coelogyne cristata* – may develop. *A. bulbiferum* is a graceful pendent fern with light green bracken-like fronds up to two feet long: these, too, may sprout small plantlets, from the surfaces of the fronds. *A. nidus*, the Bird's Nest Fern, so called because the tall (two to four foot) undivided fronds converge at the base in a tight nest-like rosette, has stiff but elegant bright shining green fronds with a prominent dark spine, and there is a variety with crinkly fronds.

Some *Blechnum* species display themselves well by providing their own pedestal – a short, often quite thick, woody trunk. *Blechnum brasiliense** and *B. gibbum* are handsome, if rather large plants, their trunks eighteen inches and two to three feet high respectively, with oblong, divided fronds up to three feet long. *B. lanceolatum* is similar but a smaller plant altogether with fronds six to twelve inches long.

Other good ferns for pots or urns are *Cyrtomium* species, generally with large, arched, firm-stemmed fronds simply divided into pairs of rather leathery, shining evergreen leaves (*Cyrtomium falcatum* is particularly tolerant of draughts and fumes); *Polypodium*, also with simply divided fronds, usually evergreen, those of *Polypodium glaucophyllum* being a glaucous blue-green; and *Pteris*, a variable genus in size, colour and shape, in which a number of species and varieties are variegated with creamy or silver-white markings. *Pteris cretica*, the Ribbon Fern, is perhaps the best known species, and the curious crested *P. cretica sempervirens* should be noted.

Many *Davallia*, with their pretty, finely divided fronds anything from four inches to four feet long according to species, are perfect for hanging pots or baskets (*D. canariensis* is a particularly successful species indoors). So also are *Nephrolepsis* (Sword Ferns); *Nephrolepsis exaltata* has stiff, feathery fronds up to three feet long, but there are smaller, more compact varieties such as *maasii*, *wredei compacta* and *bostoniensis*, the Boston Fern. *Polypodium subauriculatum* is another good, though large, basket fern.

Some of the best climbing ferns for the conservatory (they need high temperatures and humidity) are in the genus *Lygodium*, which climb by wrapping their stems around their support. The divided, often branching fronds continue to grow throughout the fern's life – and in their natural habitat may reach a hundred feet long. The best species of more suitable proportions are *Lygodium scandens* var. *microphyllum*, and *L. circinatum** whose fronds are somewhat similar in shape to the leaves of *Passiflora caerulea*.

The genus *Platycerium* (Staghorn Ferns) is so unlike one's conventional notion of a fern that we have left it to the end. They are exotic plants, some might even say sinister-looking, and a large specimen grown alone in a hanging basket can be very dramatic; or a smaller specimen makes an effective contribution to a mixed group of plants, possibly around a pool.

Their fronds vary in colour from quite a bright, fresh green to a dull, almost blue-grey green. Size is really a matter of choice for although the fronds may reach four or five feet in length (up to seventeen feet in their natural habitat), small plants can be bought and they are slow growers. Each plant has two types of leaf: the large, leathery, roughly triangular fronds, irregularly forked and often furry like young stag's antlers, and the smaller, saucer-shaped leaves at their base. The latter are infertile but their convex form covers and protects the root stock from drying out, also allowing humus and moisture to collect between the roots and the bark or other surface on which these epiphytic ferns grow.

Staghorn Ferns can be grown in pots indoors but, to our mind, they are infinitely better displayed packed with sphagnum moss in a hanging basket or fastened to a block of wood.

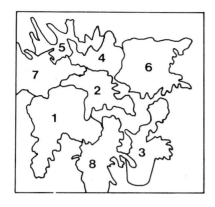

123. (ferns) *Platycerium bifurcatum*

124. *Ferns* mixed:
    Adiantum pubescens (syn. *A. hispidulum*) (1)
    A. scutum roseum (2)
    Asplenium bulbiferum (3)
    A. nidus (4)
    Nephrolepsis exaltata (5)
    Polypodium glaucum (6)
    Pteris umbrosa (7)
    P. poweri (8)

123

124

They are not difficult to grow – in fact *Platycerium bifurcatum* and its slightly more erect, finely divided form *alcicorne* seem as tough as elephant hide and put up with considerable neglect. To flourish, however, the roots must be kept moist and the plants welcome a periodic thorough drenching. An occasional fertilizer is also appreciated. Other species such as *P. grande* and *P. hillii* require tropical conditions.

As to fern culture in general, the individual requirements of all the various species and varieties mentioned above vary so greatly that we cannot give more than general information here: anyone buying new plants should find out as much as possible from their supplier and/or consult a monograph on the subject. The ferns mentioned here range from some, such as a number of the aspleniums and blechnums, that are quite tolerant of room conditions, to others that must have a high degree of humidity and be protected very carefully from draughts, fumes etc. Some do not mind the sun but it is as

well to keep them all out of the direct rays because those that are susceptible can be badly damaged or killed; care must also be taken with syringing and overhead watering as the foliage of some can suffer badly from standing moisture. In general, as might be expected, the more delicate and filmy the foliage appears the less tolerant the species is.

Most of the ferns referred to should be potted in leaf mould with charcoal added and some in peat and sharp sand, also with charcoal. They do not on the whole like being potted hard.

Propagation may be by sowing spores, by root division, by pegging down runners or detaching and planting the plantlets where these are produced.

* These species really prefer tropical conditions: high humidity and a minimum temperature of 15° (59°F).

Ficus

Ficus carica, the common, fruit-bearing, deciduous fig tree is not of course suitable as a house plant but a number of evergreen members of this varied genus make elegant foliage plants.

The deservedly most popular, *F. elastica*, the Indiarubber Plant, has smooth, regular, large oblong, dark green leaves. In its natural surroundings it will grow up to a hundred feet but it is usually bought as a plant about one foot high which, if kept pot-bound and only occasionally fed with fertilizers, is easily manageable. It can be kept single-stemmed and a young plant may need the support of a stick to keep it straight or the leaf-bud may be pinched out, in late April or early May at the start of new growth, when it will form branches that can be ornamentally trained.

The plants are tough but, as others, not fool-proof. Over- and under-watering will do harm. If a plant has been over-watered the leaves will become discoloured; if it has been allowed to dry out too much the lower leaves will drop off. In the case of the former the plant should be allowed to dry out completely before watering is again started.

In winter the plants have a dormant period when they should be kept on the dry side until new shoots start again. If the youngest leaves are small and wrinkled this means that the plant needs fertilizing or else re-potting although, in general, plants do not mind being quite severely pot-bound. The rose-coloured sheath enclosing new leaves should be watched and be removed if it is cramping growth, otherwise the leaf may be distorted or rot. It is best to allow new growth to take place out of the direct sun when the leaves will be more luxuriant.

At all times, both for the sake of their health and for their looks the leaves of the plants should be regularly sponged, preferably with milk diluted with water.

The original *F. elastica* is now seldom sold. Instead the variety *F. elastica* 'Decora', a better plant, is offered. Another variety, 'Doescheri', has variegated markings of pink and cream on the leaves, as does the variety 'Tricolor'.

The following species of *Ficus* are also worth noting. The large leafed *F. benghalensis* or Banyan Tree which branches naturally when quite young; it is very tough and will grow continuously provided that the temperature stays above 10° (50°F). *F. benjamina* which does not look like a fig but forms a small elegant tree with long smooth green leaves on slender, drooping branches; it will grow quite fast without needing much light. *F. deltoidea* (syn. *diversifolia*), the Mistletoe Fig, that produces small red or yellow berries and has small round-ish leaves; it likes a moist atmosphere and should not be allowed to dry out. *F. lyrata*, the Banjo, or Fiddle-leaf Fig, with large, very leathery leaves. *F. microcarpa* (sometimes wrongly called *F. retusa* or *F. nitida*) is rather similar to *F. benjamina* but without the pendent habit. *F. montana* (syn. *quercifolia*), a small shrub which looks like a miniature oak tree. *F. pumila*, an almost hardy, ivy-like trailer with small heart-shaped leaves,* and *F. radicans variegata* with long, variegated leaves are interesting mainly as examples of the diversity of this genus; the former prefers the shade and neither should be allowed to dry out.

All these species will fruit.

Red spider is the main enemy of *Ficus* and as usual is best prevented by syringing, but scale insects may also attack the larger-leaved species.

Cuttings need a temperature of 25° (77°F) or a few degrees more to root successfully.

* This species is perhaps best with a soil mix No. 3.

125. *Ficus elastica* 'Decora'

126. *Ficus pumila*

127. *Ficus radicans variegata*

128. *Ficus benjamina*

125

126

127

128

Fittonia

A plant admired for its foliage: the flowers are insignificant and the buds can be pinched out. The veins of the leaves are delicately traced – in the case of *Fittonia argyroneura* in white and of *F. verschaffeltii* in deep red.

Fittonias are particularly demanding of tropical rain forest conditions. *F. argyroneura*, in fact, should only be acquired if something close to these can be provided but *F. verschaffeltii* is less exacting. The former is a small plant and the latter quite a fast growing trailer.

It is particularly important to ensure that plants are neither over- nor under-watered.

Fortunella

The Kumquats, a small genus of trees closely related to citruses, make delightful house plants with handsome foliage, frequent crops of fragrant white flowers and small orange- or lemon-shaped fruit: *if* they have been successfully started. *Fortunella japonica* with small spherical, golden-yellow fruit and *F. margarita*, with lemon-shaped, yellowish-red fruit are the species most usually found.

Cultivation and habits are similar to those of *Citrus* (q.v.).

New plants are formed by grafting onto stock of *Poncirus trifoliata* or *Citrus limon*; and it is of course very important that this initial operation should have been accomplished successfully, otherwise the plants will be weedy or revert to the stock.

Freesia

The delightful scent and grace of freesias make them particularly worth growing as house plants. Moreover they are not difficult except that they positively dislike the high temperatures so essential for most flowering house plants and must be kept in a cool place, 10–15° (50–59°F) until they are in bud. There are numerous hybrids in a variety of colours and shades, such as creamy white, yellow, deep rose, mauve, etc.

Freesias can be grown from seed but, in this context, are more easily grown from the corm stage. Corms should be well developed and planted about an inch apart in pots; they should be covered with half an inch of soil and the drainage must be good. They are best planted from August until October and stood outside until there is danger of frost. If the temperature is allowed to rise much above 15° (59°F) before the buds have formed there is a strong likelihood of the plants being blind. The flower shoots need support (from sticks with raffia or thread) or they may bend and be damaged.

Fortnightly feeding should be started when the flower buds appear and be continued until the leaves start to die because the period after flowering, as with most corms and bulbs, is crucial, to enable them to gain strength for the following year. Once the leaves are dead, watering should stop and the pots or corms be stored, dry, until the next season.

If planted in clean soil and well cared for freesias should not suffer from disease. The corms however may be attacked by dry rot or by wilt, which appear, in the first case, as brown patches turning to black and in the second as red patches or spots near the root base. In the case of wilt the leaves also start to yellow from the tips and the outer leaves may turn brown and die. Any corms so affected must be destroyed and the others carefully inspected (to the extent of peeling off the scales) to make sure that they are healthy. Lastly, there is a virus disease, Mosaic, which shows as patches of yellow on the leaves, gradually turning to white: affected plants should immediately be destroyed.

Fritillaria – see BULBS

129

130

131

132

Fuchsia

Fuchsias are awkward plants for the house because they demand conditions that are not only difficult to achieve but also that clash with the requirements of most other summer-flowering house plants – maximum light and high humidity together with a cool temperature, certainly not higher than 20° (68°F) and lower if possible. Furthermore, they are deciduous, with a long dormant period.

However they produce such strikingly handsome flowers that many will nonetheless yield to the temptation and try to create a suitable place for them indoors. The flowers are tubular or bell-shaped, the calyx usually being one or another shade of red or white and the petals purplish-blue or white.

There are so many varieties and hybrids available that it is best to take your choice from what the suppliers have on offer,

although be sure to check that the chosen plant will withstand indoor conditions. If you want to concentrate on fuchsias it is essential to have a monograph on the subject for guidance. Many hybrids are suitable for training as standards and so make excellent, long-flowering conservatory plants. One species, *F. procumbens*, is worth picking out because it is relatively hardy and, having a creeping habit, is excellent for a hanging basket. The flowers face upwards and are pale orange, with purple-tipped lobes and pale blue anthers; they are followed by purplish red berries.

Fuchsias are prone to a number of pests such as mealy bug, red spider mite and white fly.

Galanthus – see BULBS

Gardenia

The impact of the numerous white, intensely fragrant flowers against their background of glossy green leaves gives the gardenia pre-eminence among house plants. It is not easy to bring into flower each year but is no more difficult than are many other flowering house plants and the rewards of success are so great that it is abundantly worth trying so long as you are confident of providing the essential requirements.

Throughout the budding and flowering season a gardenia must have plenty of light (although the buds will wilt temporarily if exposed to a high temperature with inadequate ventilation), a temperature of about 20–25° (68–77°F) by day and not much below 15° (59°F) by night, and, very important, high humidity. Also important, gardenias need strongly acid soil with a high content of iron which they will quickly use up: thus they should be fertilized every six weeks during the growth season with sequestrene (iron chelate) or a similar formula;* in addition, Elbert and Hyams suggest an occasional dose of sulphate of ammonia (one teaspoonful to the gallon). Other, balanced, organic fertilizers should be given frequently during this season.

It is essential also to allow all but the most mature plants a good period of rest – some six months – after flowering or the tendency will be for them to sprout more and more feeble buds which will lead to a general decline in the capacity of a plant to give a good show of flowers; in the case of *Gardenia jasminoides* it is best to start pinching out immediately after the peak of flowering has been reached and allow another flowering season in five to six months. Mature plants – say over seven years old – will however produce good flowers almost throughout the year.

After all this has been said, probably the most crucial piece of advice is to ensure that you get a good, robust plant in the first place. The best time to buy is when the plant is in bud. The buds should be full and the leaves glossily healthy. If you can then make sure that you can provide conditions similar to those in which the plant has been kept you have every likelihood of success. One is usually advised to concentrate on younger plants because they give larger flowers but we have found that good plants will continue to flower excellently for a number of years. (The most splendid *G. jasminoides* that we have seen was one, some fifteen feet high and the same width, grafted onto *Syringa* stock;** it produces an almost continuous succession of magnificent, large flowers.)

Cuttings should be of young shoots with a heel.

The varieties of *G. jasminoides* that flower in the summer are those most likely to do well; *G. globosa* is also lovely and some will be tempted by one of the most exotic of all plants, *G. thunbergia*, which flowers in early summer. It is a fast grower but unlikely to flower until several years old. Cuttings of *G. thunbergia* do not take easily and seed is a surer method.

G. jasminoides is prone to several pests and should be sprayed periodically with a systemic insecticide; similarly *G. thunbergia* whose new growth is liable to be attacked by scale insects.

* Ballard, *Garden in your House*, New York, revised edition, 1971, p. 150, writes that gardenias have a 'constitutional inability to absorb iron from the soil when grown at temperature below 60°F.' (*c*. 15°).
** In the collection of King's Exotic Flowers, New York.

Gasteria

Gasteria is a genus of succulent or semi-succulent plants closely related to *Aloe*. They are valued for their usually symmetrical foliage; the small, long-stemmed flowers are secondary. Most species are quite small and take up little room.

Although plants will thrive better in good light and the colouring of the leaves will benefit, they are quite toughly resistant to adverse conditions.

The illustration of *G. subverrucosa* shows an inflorescence that has been crossed with three other *Gasteria* species. Each colour of wool represents a separate cross.*

* We are very grateful to Dr P. E. Brandham of Kew for allowing us to photograph his work.

133

134

135

133. *Gardenia thunbergia*

134. *Gardenia jasminoides*

135. *Gasteria subverrucosa*

Gelsemium

A twining warm-climate shrub that is well worth cultivating. *Gelsemium sempervirens*, Caroline Yellow Jessamine or False Jasmine, is the best known species with exotic, large, fragrant, tubular yellow flowers; there is another, *G. rankinii*, that is very similar.

Plants should be watched for attacks by mealy bug and red spider mite.

Gerbera

Gerbera jamesonii, the best species, appears frequently in the form of beautiful cut flowers of various colours, not so often as a pot plant.

G. jamesonii can be raised from seed but plants do not reach their best until the third year. They should not be over-potted or over-watered; the latter may cause foot rot which should be treated immediately with sulphur powder or such like.

They are also very prone to attacks by pests, specifically white fly and leaf miner, the latter being particularly virulent. However, no insecticide containing azobenzene or malathion should be used lest the plants are damaged* and the best remedies are gamma-BHC, diazinon or parathion.

* Royal Horticultural Society's *Dictionary of Gardening, Supplement*, p. 326.

Gesneria

Some confusion has surrounded this genus and a number of tuberous-rooted plants that were classified as *Gesneria* have now been transferred to *Rechsteineria*. Those species that remain within the genus are fibrous-rooted.

Gesneria albiflora, with tubular cream-coloured flowers, shading almost to yellow, and *G. citrina* with yellow flowers,

are both worth cultivating because they bloom in the winter (the latter flowers throughout the year). *G. albiflora* is quite a large shrub, growing as tall as four feet, but *G. citrina* is more compact. *G. cuneifolia*, with bright red flowers, is also attractive but it needs 85–90% humidity and so is unlikely to be a practical proposition except in a terrarium.

Gloriosa

A small genus of strikingly beautiful climbing plants. *Gloriosa superba* and *G. rothschildiana* are probably the best species. The long, wavy, swept-back petals of the former are orange and red or sometimes pure yellow, and of the latter deep red shading to yellow at the base or pure yellow also.

The tubers, which should be as large as possible, (some five inches long) to ensure flowering, should be planted in 6-inch pots from February to the end of March; the temperature

should be as close to 20° (68°F) as possible and certainly not below 15° (59°F).

Once growth has started plants will benefit from plenty of water and feeding. After flowering, when they begin to die back, watering should be continued for a while to strengthen the tubers but finally withheld; and the pots should be stored dry in a temperature not below 10° (50°F) until the following season.

Gloxinia – see SINNINGIA *speciosa*

136. *Gelsemium sempervirens*

137. *Gerbera jamesonii*

138. *Gesneria cardinalis* (top red), with *Streptocarpus* (blue)

139. *Gloriosa superba*

140. *Grevillea × semperflorens*

Grevillea

The Australian *Grevillea* is widely known through the species *G. robusta* which is a tree that will grow to a hundred feet or more in its native habitat. When young its branching, delicate green, feathery leaves make it a most attractive foliage plant that contrasts beautifully with some of the more squat, broad-leafed foliage plants.

G. robusta's yellowish-orange flowers are 'rarely or never seen in Britain'.* There are, however, other species that make quite compact, though largish, shrubs that do flower and moreover may do so in winter. The small tubular flowers with prominent style are quietly attractive and particularly welcome at a rather barren time of year. *G. alpina*, whose flowers are red, shading to cream, is one of the most satisfactory, because compact, shrubs, but *G. × semperflorens*, though larger, with yellow flowers shading to white and with prominent pink style is also well worth cultivating.

G. robusta is prone to attacks of red spider mite.

* Royal Horticultural Society's *Dictionary of Gardening*, Vol. II, p. 932.

Guzmania

rosette

osmunda
+
No. 1

Together with the better known *Tillandsia* and *Vriesia*, *Guzmania* is one of the three most striking of the 'flowering' bromeliads.

Guzmania monostachya (syn. *G. tricolor*) is perhaps the most spectacular, with its long, erect scape of small white flowers, cupped in yellow-green bracts streaked with black and tipped with bright red; but the more readily available *G. sanguinea* and *G. zahnii* (syns. *Caraguata sanguinea* and *C. zahnii*), both with numerous, short-lived yellow flowers in the rosette and

in panicles respectively, are very fine. The last two species also have conspicuously coloured foliage.

Like *Aechmea*, a rosette that has produced a flower will gradually die off but offsets should be produced, although there may be an interval of several months between the dying of the flower and the appearance of offsets: so it is best to be patient and not throw the plant away precipitately.

For general instructions see *Aechmea*.

Gynura

No. 1

Although *Gynura aurantiaca* and *G. sarmentosa*, the most useful species, have small orange flowers, these plants are valued primarily for their foliage. *G. aurantiaca* may have rather plain green leaves or, in one form, violet hairs covering its leaves and stems, especially the young ones, while *G. sarmentosa*, also known as *G. scandens*, has slate-blue leaves, a shade of purple below and tinged with purple above. The hairs on the

leaves create a dramatic purple iridescence at certain angles when the sun shines on them.

Both species are rapid growers and can be pinched back if a compact plant is wanted and also to prevent small leaves developing which tend to be the concomitant of rapid growth.

They should be kept rather dry in cool conditions.

Haemanthus

No. 3

Not such graceful plants as some of the other Amaryllidaceae because the flower stems of most species are rather short and thick but this is compensated for by spectacularly large umbels of flowers in various shades of red and orange, or white. The large leaves appear after the flowers and subsequently die back.

Haemanthus coccineus is perhaps the most satisfactory species but there are other attractive species, varieties and hybrids available.

Bulbs are best planted in the spring with their necks just above the surface of moist soil and full watering should only begin

when the shoots appear. As with hippeastrums and similar bulbous plants it is what happens immediately after flowering that conditions the next season's performance: the bulbs must be given plenty of light and heat so that their strength is fully restored, and then rested until they show renewed signs of growth.

Haemanthus seem none the worse for being somewhat pot-bound and should only need repotting every three years.

141

143

142

141. *Guzmania zahnii*

142. *Gynura aurantiaca*
(purple form) – See
also in *Asparagus*
group, plate 22.

143. *Haemanthus
katherinae*

Haworthia   No.2

A large genus of small succulent plants, closely related to *Aloe*, with leaves in the shape of a rosette or a close spiral. The small flowers on a thin stem are of little interest. They are quite easy plants and more probably at their best when grouped with other succulents or cacti.

A number of species such as *Haworthia coarctata*, *H. fasciata* and *H. papillosa* have curious white nodules on their leaves;

as does the formally attractive spiral-shaped *H. reinwardtii*.

A period out of doors during the summer suits them. They should be re-potted every one to two years in the autumn because the old roots die and turn the soil sour.

They are very prone to mealy bug and so must always be watched carefully.

Hedera   No.3

Ivies are among the easiest, least demanding house plants: hence their popularity, because they are not usually very exciting. Most can be used as climbers or as trailers and can contribute to a grouping of plants or, better, can be grown large and be incorporated into the design or structure of a room; many can for instance be trained along bamboos or suchlike to divide a kitchen from a dining-room.

Hedera canariensis and *H. helix* with its numerous varieties

and cultivars, of single-coloured or variegated foliage, are the species most commonly found.

Plants survive with a minimum of the usual care but they should not be overpotted and, if they are to give of their limited best, should have their foliage sponged quite often. They benefit from a spell outdoors in the summer but this is by no means essential – nor, if they have been trained up some structure, possible.

Hedychium   No.3

Although this genus belongs to the versatile ginger family, Zingiberaceae, it has the appearance of a lily. The delicate white flowers, sometimes tinged with yellow, of *Hedychium coronarium*, or the white shading into yellow and deep orange flowers of the even more gorgeous *H. chrysoleucum*, perhaps a variety of *H. coronarium*, are delightfully fragrant. In fact this is one of the less well known genera that we recommend most strongly to the ambitious collector.

Moreover, some hedychiums are nearly hardy, although the more exotic, such as those mentioned above, thrive under

tropical conditions with plenty of water (while growing they should be stood in two or three inches of water which should ideally be warm). They also need to be heavily fertilized.

The only disadvantage is that the plants tend to grow rather large – from four to six feet: they can be cut back to within some two feet of the ground after flowering. Plants should be re-potted in larger pots in the second year and you can at that point divide the rhizomes. One warning: the rhizomes obtainable are unlikely to be mature enough to produce flowers in the first year.

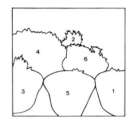

144. *Haworthia* mixed:
    H. asperuscula (1)
    H. altenata (2)
    H. cuspidata (3)
    H. cymbiflormis (4)
    H. tesselata (5)
    H. tortuosa (6)

145. *Hedera* mixed:
    H. helix 'Glacier' (1)
    H. helix 'Chicago'
    cristata (2)
    H. canariensis (3)
    H. 'Adam' (sport) (4)
    H. 'Eva' (5)
    H. 'Adam' (6)
    H. helix marmorata (7)
    H. helix 'Golden
    Chicago' (8)

146. *Hedychium gardnerianum*

144

145

146

95

Heliotropium

Both *Heliotropium corymbosum* and *H. peruvianum* are quite easy as house plants and well worth growing because of their lovely scent.

In their growth they are adaptable plants and can be pinched back to make compact shrubs or trained to become standards. Moreoever they can be held back to flower in the winter although they will need a lot of light to do so. When not in growth plants should be kept on the dry side.

If cuttings are taken this should be done with vigorous young shoots in the spring or mid-summer. Young plants do better than old and so, if possible, a constant supply should be kept up. Tarsonemid mites may appear and show themselves by brown patches on the young leaves. Dicofol, endrin or endosulfan should deal with them.

Helxine *soleirolii* – see SOLEIROLIA *soleirolii*

Hibiscus

Hibiscus can be one of the greatest delights of the indoor plant lover as the large-flowered species, particularly when the flowers are single with spectacular stamens, have a breath-taking tropical splendour. Each flower may last as little as a day but a healthy plant will flower abundantly throughout a long season; in fact you can have flowers all the year round if you can provide enough heat and light.

What is more, hibiscus is not difficult provided that you follow the basic guide-lines that apply to all flowering shrubs or trees from the wet tropics. Hibiscus flourish in a temperature of 15–25° (59–77°F) but will tolerate going down to 10° (50°F), as much sun and light as possible, with liberal watering and syringing but good drainage. The reward will be a constant series of exquisite blooms. When the temperature is low, moisture must be decreased, otherwise the roots will be damaged and the leaves will yellow and drop. If this does happen take immediate remedial action and new shoots will soon form. Plants can be pruned if they become straggly and this will encourage more abundant flowering.

Because growers tend for economic reasons to pot-bind plants acutely, we have found it wise to re-pot new plants immediate-ly they have been bought. This is very easily done and will not set the plant back at all even if it is in full bud. Some growers have recently adopted the irritating practice of offering two little plants in a pot to create a more abundant-looking package. In this case they should be re-potted as above, but not separated and planted in individual pots until after the first flowering season.

The only drawback to this delightful plant is its proneness to green fly on the buds. The only remedy is frequent spraying with an aerosol or liquid insecticide.

Thanks to the enterprise of a few growers hibiscus is now quite widely available in a number of species and varieties, usually with pink, orange or yellow flowers. Most of those offered are varieties of *Hibiscus rosa-sinensis*, of which one, *cooperi*, has rather gaudy green leaves blotched with cream and crimson. Unfortunately *H. schizopetalus*, an exquisite pendulous hibiscus with delicate, sinuous red flowers, is not generally available. It would make an ideal plant for the hanging basket.

147. *Heliotropium peruvianum*

148. *Hibiscus* 'Lee Orange'

148

Hippeastrum

Magnificent bulbous pot plants, belonging to the Amaryllidaceae. The bulbs give forth umbels of some three to six splendid, usually large flowers on long stalks; and there may be several successive stalks. Some of the species have very gracefully shaped flowers, such as *Hippeastrum aulicum* (crimson), *H. blumenavia* (white with mauve-crimson markings) or *H. pratense* (bright scarlet, yellow at base). A number of growers have been very active in the creation of hybrids but unfortunately those most widely offered show an emphasis on the size of bloom at the expense of shape which can make them almost overwhelmingly florid, although, in compensation, some fine and delicate colours and colour combinations have been developed.

The leaves will usually appear after the flowers which is a pity because the plant then presents an inelegant nudity.

It is best to buy bulbs that have retained their roots although these will have dried out. Some people advise one to place a newly bought bulb on a jar or vase of water with the roots in the water for 24 to 48 hours before planting and this seems to work well. The bulbs should also be carefully examined for any sign of mealy bugs and should have any dead roots or decayed parts removed (in the latter case the wound should be dusted with sulphur powder). They should be planted in pots of a size that gives about an inch between the bulb and the rim of the pot; the pot should have good drainage and the soil be sprinkled carefully into it so that it does not become too packed and so as to avoid damaging the roots. The bulbs

should only be one-third to a half covered with soil. They should be well watered in but then kept almost dry until the bud starts to grow. It is essential not to allow water to lodge in the crown of the bulb, or rot will set in.

Hippeastrums can be planted at any time of the year. They will do best in a temperature of at least 15° (59°F) and do not seem to mind dry heat, e.g. from central heating. If they are started in a bottom heat of some 20° (68°F) results will be speedier but this is in no way necessary.

After flowering they need maximum light and plenty of water, as well as feeding so that the bulbs are restored, as they will have been somewhat exhausted by flowering.

By August-September they will be ready for their dormant period and can be allowed to dry out (in which case they will lose their leaves).

Bulbs can be left for a couple of years in a pot. When the time to re-pot comes – from December onwards – the offsets should be detached from the main bulb and, if more plants are required, planted separately in smaller, say 4-inch, pots. These should flower after two or three years.

Hippeastrums are prone to spotted wilt (pale yellow or whitish spots on the leaves), thrips and red spider mite. If they are inadequately drained or over-watered they may also suffer from basal rot.

Hoffmannia

The most usually available species, *Hoffmannia ghiesbreghtii*, has inconspicuous little yellow flowers and is valued primarily for its curious foliage. Its large crinkly leaves are a deep velvety green above and purplish beneath.

Care should be taken to ensure that dust does not collect in the

leaves' crinkles and the plant should therefore periodically be held upside down and sprayed quite vigorously with, if possible, rainwater.

There are other species with rather more attractive flowers.

Homocladium *platycladum* – see MUEHLENBECKIA *platyclados*

149

149. *Hippeastrum × johnsoni*

150. *Hoffmannia ghiesbreghtii*

150

Hoya

Belongs to the same family, the Asclepiadaceae, as the rather more spectacular *Stephanotis*. *Hoya carnosa*, the most popular species, is quite an attractive plant; the waxy leaves are more pointed and do not die off in the winter as may those of stephanotis. The plant is seen at its best from below – when trained, say, across a conservatory roof so that the closely packed pendent umbels of small pinkish white flowers are more easily enjoyed. Never remove flower stems because these will continue to produce flowers from year to year but the main shoot can be pinched out to produce more lateral stems to flower later.

Hoya bella is a more delicate, dwarf, shrubby species that is good in hanging baskets. It is probably best given a No. 1 soil mix. Its white flowers have a purple centre and also hang down – usually with a drop of glistening nectar at the centre.

Hoyas are prone to mealy bugs but otherwise are tough.

Propagation can be by layering or by shoots of the previous year's growth taken in the spring.

Humea

Humea elegans is a graceful, tall plant with numerous tiny flowers, in shades of red or pink, hanging from its tree-like branches. The leaves, when stroked, give off a curious scent.

The plant is biennial and should be raised from seed sown under glass in April to July for flowering some fifteen months later. Plants should be discarded after flowering.

Hyacinthus – see BULBS

Hydrangea

Most varieties of *Hydrangea macrophylla* are hardy and can be grown outside provided they are sheltered from the extreme cold but they also make popular and easy pot plants.

They need as much light as possible, but no great warmth. When in growth they must have plenty of water and they respond well to feeding; they should never be allowed to dry out. Growers offer them with flowers in various shades of pink or blue, or white.

Plants in pots are usually offered for sale when coming into flower. After flowering is over it is best to cut out the old wood and allow new shoots to develop from the base of the plant. Only the best three or four such shoots should be retained, any others being cut back. Plants will benefit from being stood outside for the rest of the summer but should be brought in before there is danger of frost. They will shed their leaves in the winter and during this period should be kept only just moist in a cool atmosphere. As soon as new leaf buds start to appear (or before that, if you want to force the plant) a higher temperature – about 15° (59°F) – and increased watering should be provided. It may at this point be advisable to transfer the plant to a larger pot taking care not to damage the fibrous or the tap roots.

To retain the colour in blue-flowered plants or to turn pink- to blue-flowered plants, aluminium sulphate should be added to the soil when re-potting and again at the end of the flowering season; $\frac{3}{4}$ oz of ground crystals should be mixed in with the soil of a 5-inch pot and $1\frac{1}{2}$ ozs in a 6-inch pot, or else a commercially marketed colorant can be used. If the reverse process is wanted the soil should be allowed to become less acid. White-flowered hydrangeas cannot be changed to another colour (except by a process similar to that used by the gardeners in *Alice in Wonderland*). If hydrangeas are given inadequate ventilation they may develop powdery mildew which can be cured by better ventilation and less humidity and, if necessary, Bordeaux mixture or a similar preparation. Hydrangeas may suffer from iron deficiency, shown in the yellowing of their leaves, in which case they should be fed with sequestrene (iron chelate). They are also subject to attacks by green capsid bugs which can be destroyed by fenitrothion.

151

151. *Hoya carnosa*

152. *Humea elegans*

153. *Hydrangea* 'Blue Wave'

152

153

Hymenocallis

One of the most beautiful of the Amaryllidaceae, closely related to *Ismene*. The evergreen *Hymenocallis speciosa* has lovely fragrant white flowers in the form of thin graceful outer petals radiating round an inner cup. There are a number of other attractive species, all with white flowers except for two, *H. amancaes* and *H. × spofforthiae*, that have yellow ones and are deciduous. They require varying degrees of heat; *H. speciosa*, for instance, at one end of the scale, needs warmth throughout the year whereas some species may be grown outdoors.

Bulbs should be planted with their necks above the surface of the soil and there should be plenty of room in the pot for root growth. The evergreen species need to be kept moist throughout the year but the deciduous ones should be allowed to dry out during the winter.

Hypocyrta

Of this genus *Hypocyrta glabra* is the species most widely offered for sale as a house plant. Its small dark green shiny leaves and the smaller orange flowers do not make it an outstandingly attractive plant but it is undemanding and can be useful as a hanging or semi-hanging plant.

Any pruning should be done before the new growth starts because it is on this that the flower buds will form.

Hypoestes

Hypoestes sanguinolenta is an evergreen plant valued both for its foliage – downy dark green leaves spotted with pink as if paint had been spilled over them – and for its pale purple and white flowers. It is liable to become straggly but can be ruthlessly pruned. In fact it is best to create a constant supply of new plants by cutting off shoots which will root easily and quickly.

H. taeniata is another species worth cultivating because of its curious, delicately wavy, tubular, purple flowers with red calyces.

Hypoestes are prone to attacks by scale insects.

Impatiens

The sight of an inadequately cared for *Impatiens wallerana*, *petersiana* or *sultani* with ugly straggling stems from which the lower leaves have fallen is apt to prejudice one against this plant. Nor do the vapid leaves and the rather hideous fuchsia-colour of the most usual species' flowers endear it.

However there are now numerous hybrids and varieties with a wide range of far more attractively coloured flowers – other, richer shades of red, yellow, etc. – and also darker, less insipid foliage. This, coupled with the fact that plants will flower in abundance almost continuously throughout the winter, should more than overcome any prejudice against it. The dwarf *I. jerdoniae* makes a useful hanging plant and dwarf forms of *I. wallerana* have also been developed.

Exposure to draughts or too dry an atmosphere will hasten the yellowing and dropping of the lower leaves. If this happens the plants should be cut back at a relatively less active stage and allowed to re-sprout.

Cuttings can also be taken at any time, to replace ungainly plants. They will root easily and the only danger is rotting off from too much moisture.

Impatiens is frequently attacked by green fly, white fly and red spider mites. Malathion should not be used as it is liable to cause damage.

154. *Hymenocallis caribaea*

155. *Hypocyrta glabra*

156. *Hypoestes phyllostachoca*

157. *Impatiens petersiana*

154

155

156

157

Ipomoea

A genus of twining plants of which Morning Glory, *Ipomoea tricolor* (syn. *Pharbitis tricolor*) is perhaps the best known. This is an annual that does best out of doors.

Ipomoea learii (syn. *Pharbitis learii*), the Blue Dawn-flower, on the other hand, is an evergreen twiner with handsome leaves and a mass of bright blue flowers like those of Morning Glory. It is somewhat rampant but well worth having if there is room. It can be cut back at will at any time.

Ipomoea learii has vigorous roots and should therefore be given a large pot – at least eight inches.

Iris – see BULBS

Isoloma – see KOHLERIA

Ixia

A genus in the iris family, *Ixia* contains a number of delightful species and varieties. The star-shaped flowers are in a wide range of colour, usually with a darker centre; *Ixia viridiflora* is notable for having blue-green flowers with nearly black eyes.

The corms should be planted several to a pot in October and kept in a cool place until the spring when they should be moved to a somewhat warmer, light, airy position and the watering should be increased when the flower spikes appear.

Watering should be continued until the leaves have died back when the pots should be dried out and laid in the sun so that the corms may ripen. They should be kept dry until October when the process should be repeated (cf. *Freesia*).

Ixora

A large genus of evergreen shrubs or trees. The clusters, or corymbs, of flowers look as if they should be delightfully scented. Unfortunately most species have no scent but *Ixora acuminata*, *I. finlaysoniana*, *I. laxiflora* and *I. odorata* are fragrant. These, then, can be particularly recommended and even the unscented species have a quiet, neat attraction; they have moreover a long flowering season. The flowers, according to species, may be white, yellow, orange, pink or red.

The branches of the plants can be trimmed back to about one joint after flowering, for compactness and to get a better crop of flowers next year.

Ixoras demand maximum light, and a high temperature coupled with a high degree of humidity, to flourish.

158

158. *Ipomoea learii*

159. *Ixia* mixed

160. *Ixora* mixed:
     I. coccinea 'Henry
     North' (left)
     I. chinensis (right),

159

160

Jacaranda

One of the most beautiful tropical and sub-tropical genera of shrubs or trees, both for their elegant acacia-like foliage and for their lovely mauve or blue panicles of flowers. The genus derives from Brazil but trees prosper magnificently in Portugal, Sicily, South Africa and other such countries, as well as in areas of the rainy tropics.

Jacarandas are fast-growing and some soon become much too large for indoors. *Jacaranda mimosifolia* (the correct name for *J. ovalifolia*) may, however, only grow to about ten feet under cultivation and will stand quite rigorous pruning – in the late winter. It is in fact a good idea to nip off the top of a young plant when it has reached a height of, say, two feet; otherwise it may do no more than provide a decreasingly graceful umbrella of foliage (the lower leaves will almost inevitably die away).

Plenty of water should be given during hot weather. Plants are tender in their first year but thereafter will tolerate a temperature down to 10° (50°F).

Cuttings of half-ripe shoots will root in the spring or summer but plants can well be raised from seed which is likely to be much more easily obtainable and should germinate quickly.

Jacobinia

Those jacobinias that flower in late summer may yield to the heavy competition at that time, but a few such as *Jacobinia ghiesbreghtiana*, *J. pauciflora* and the larger flowered hybrid between these species, *J. × penrhosiensis*, are welcome for their (crimson to bright orange) winter flowers.

Plants are apt to become straggly and early leaf buds can be nipped out to produce a better shaped plant. In any event most species should be well cut back after flowering: an exception is *J. pauciflora* which should be left unpruned unless it becomes too leggy or unshapely. *J. ghiesbreghtiana* will flower much better if left out in the sun at mid-summer.

Jacobinias are particularly prone to red spider mite.

Jasminum

Jasmine is perhaps the most tantalising of plants for indoors. There can be few sights in the realm of plants more exquisite than a good *Jasminum officinale* in bud and flower; the graceful foliage, the pink-tinged buds and simple, pure white flowers are unexcelled; moreover the scent is intoxicating.

Apart from *J. officinale*, the Common Jasmine, there are *J. gracillimum* and *J. sambac*, which both flower in the winter – *sambac* almost continuously – and are very fragrant. Perhaps the most beautiful of all is the variety *multipetalum* of *J. polyanthum* with abundant, close-knit, intensely fragrant white flowers tinged with deep pink that may appear constantly for several months throughout the winter.

Alas, the bald fact has to be faced that jasmine does not take kindly to being grown indoors. Thus the superb-looking plants that one often sees in florists may give a few weeks' delight (which are well worth having) but, thereafter, unless you have a conservatory or a greenhouse, the pleasure is likely to cease because plants must have full light, a high degree of humidity, and a period out of doors during the summer for them ever to flower well again. If they do not get these conditions they will quickly grow straggly, many leaves and shoots will brown and die back and it is unlikely that much in the way of flowers will again appear.

The best hope is, naturally, to get as close as possible to the conditions that do suit jasmine. After flowering, then, as new growth starts to shoot up it should be ruthlessly nipped back; in June the plants should be re-potted in a No. 3 mix with, if possible, some well rotted manure added. Jasmine has quite a strong root system and plants bought from a florist are likely to be severely pot-bound; they should also be re-potted. The plants should then be stood in the sunniest available position, outside if at all possible, and a little but not much new growth can be allowed; during this period plants should be well watered and, from late August, fed regularly with a general fertilizer.

By September, with luck, buds should be starting to show in the leaf axils. The danger is that they may come into bud and flower outside in mid-summer so that much of the point is lost. Plants can be left outside until the end of the month, then brought in to the lightest spot, given a temperature of about 20° (68°F) and a good crop of flowers may appear in January or February. A temperature above 20° (68°F) without a compensating increase in humidity must be avoided or the buds and leaves will dry and shrivel.

Although plants can be propagated by cuttings, layering is perhaps the simpler method.

161. *Jacaranda mimosifolia* (flowers)

162. *Jacaranda mimosifolia* (foliage) with *Begonia coccinea*

163. *Jacobinia coccinea*

164. *Jasminum polyanthum*

161

162

163

164

Jatropha

A genus of plants that are thought to have medicinal properties. *Jatropha podagrica*, the Guatemala Rhubarb, is something of a curiosity as a greenhouse plant, in that it will produce, from a gouty base, a solitary long stalk with heads of bright orange-red flowers before any leaves appear; this will happen towards the end of the winter. *J. gossipifolia* is rather more conventional-looking and has panicles of striking reddish-purple flowers; it is said to provide a remedy for leprosy. *J.*

multifida, the Coral Nut or Physic Plant, has delicate, palmate leaves and scarlet flowers; *J. pandurifolia*, though somewhat larger, has the advantage of producing its cymes of scarlet flowers throughout the year.

Seeds will germinate easily with bottom heat and cuttings of firm, young shoots should be dried before planting.

Kalanchoe

The best known and most satisfactory species, *Kalanchoe blossfeldiana* has compact clusters of small scarlet flowers at the end of a six- to nine-inch stem; an unobtrusive member of the family Crassulaceae that when young takes up little space, and has the advantage of flowering in mid-winter. There are also species with yellow flowers.

Plants can easily be bought around Christmas or can be raised from seed sown in February; if the latter, they will need regular periods of intensive light and warmth from the beginning of November to encourage flowering.

Most kalanchoes are succulent and able to withstand some drought but when growing they respond best if they are well watered. They require good drainage. *K. beharensis*, which has large wavy leaves covered with fine hairs that are rust-red when young, is unlikely to flower but is valued for its foliage.

Some species of kalanchoe which were once included in the genus *Bryophyllum* have the peculiarity of sprouting plantlets from the indentations of the leaves. Some of these, such as *Kalanchoe tubiflora* and *K. daigremontiana* are often used in dish gardens.

Kohleria

Plants belonging to this genus used to be classed under *Isoloma*, a name to which a genus of ferns has prior claim.

Kohlerias are rather similar to gesnerias and rechsteinerias but, like achimenes and smithianthas, have scaly rhizomes as against fibrous roots or tubers. They differ from achimenes and smithianthas by having more tubular flowers and a five-lobed disc instead of a continuous ring.*

Some species make rather tall plants, up to three or even four feet, but the upward growing shoots can be pinched out to make a more compact plant. *Kohleria eriantha* with orange-red flowers, spotted with yellow on the lower lobes, is one of the largest species but otherwise a good plant to have. *K. bogotensis*, with red flowers shading to yellow and *K. ocellata*, a very exotic-looking plant with bright red flowers spotted with black, and white or pale yellow outlines on the lower

lobes, are well worth noting and there are a number of other species, hybrids and hybrid groups in a wide range of colours. The leaves of kohlerias are hairy, and some are ornamental.

Some kohlerias will die right down after flowering and have a dormant period like *Achimenes* (they should be similarly treated, q.v.). Others will continue to flower almost throughout the year.

Like most similar plants kohlerias are prone to attacks of thrips.

* The Royal Horticultural Society's *Dictionary of Gardening, Supplement*, 2nd edition, 1969.

165

166

167

165. *Jatropha podagrica*

166. *Kalanchoe* mixed:
    K. beharensis and
    K. blossfeldiana

167. *Kohleria* mixed:
    K. eriantha (1)
    K. bogotensis (2)
    K. amabilis (3)
    K. × amabilis (4)

Lachenalia

A genus of attractive bulbous plants of the lily family from South Africa with, usually, cowslip-like flowers on stems six or more inches high. Good bulbs will produce three or four spikes of flowers which in cool conditions last from one to two months. They must have plenty of air.

The bulbs should be planted in August two inches apart in shallow pots and covered with half an inch of soil; they should be put on a moist bed of ashes in a cool place and given a good watering, then left alone until they start to sprout, when regular watering should be started. They must have good drainage or they may develop a disease to which they are prone: a form of root rot that can be detected from a pinkish discoloration of the base of the bulb.

After flowering, put the bulbs in full sun to ripen off and leave them in the dry soil until the time comes to pot them again in August. If space is a problem, the bulbs may be removed from the soil and stored elsewhere once all the leaves have dried off.

The species *L. orchioides* is worth mentioning because its flowers, shaped rather like those of the Common Spotted Orchid and coloured whitish or yellowish, tinged with red or blue, are fragrant.

Plants are very easily increased, by seed, division or even – like *Saintpaulia* and some Gesneriads – by leaf-cuttings which quickly arrive at the flowering stage (usually within a year).

Lantana

A number of species and hybrids of lantana are adaptable, free-flowering shrubs and their clusters of verbena-like flowers, which may be lavender, pink, red, golden, white or many-coloured, will continue for several months, often into the winter.

Lantanas are natives of the tropical or semi-tropical New World and parts of Africa and Asia. However they will do well outside in Britain during the summer and can be effectively grown indoors in a hanging basket or a pot. Older plants that have been cut back flower best. Plants can also be grown into two- to three- or more foot standards. They will thrive even with little sunlight but they need to be well watered.

Lantana has a curious scent which some find exotically stimulating but others do not like.

Lapageria

Beautiful flowering vines and among the most rewarding climbing plants for indoors. The large, waxy, pendent tubular flowers may be rosy-crimson, pink or white. The white is by far the least robust and the variety *Lapageria rosea ilsemanni* is the most vigorous, with particularly striking flowers.

Lapagerias like quite a cool atmosphere and need to be shaded from direct sun in the summer but they do require plenty of water and a moist atmosphere. They should be syringed as often as possible in the flowering season.

Plants are prone to green fly and red spider mite as well as mealy bug, scale and thrips, so they should be carefully watched and treated appropriately.

Propagation may be by layering, although this is extremely difficult, as well as by seed.

168

168. *Lachenalia aloides* 'Nelsonii'

169. *Lantana camara chelsonii*

170. *Lapageria rosea* × *rosea* var. *albiflora*

169

170

Leucocoryne

A beautiful, fragrant, bulbous plant of the lily family, *Leucocoryne ixioides*, the most attractive species in the genus, has pale blue to light purple flowers in the spring. Often known as Glory of the Sun, it is well worth cultivating indoors and should be treated as for freesias (q.v.).

Lilium

This is a large genus of spectacularly flowering bulbs, many of which are quite hardy and make fine garden plants. Strictly speaking, therefore, they do not come within the terms of reference of this book. However, some of the species make excellent pot plants and, in recent years, the number of lilies so grown has been added to by the Oregon raised hybrids, an addition which has greatly increased the colour range.

Lilies are usually bought as bulbs but seed of *Lilium formosanum* is well worth trying and, unlike most lilies, may produce plants which flower in their first year. This species is very similar to *L. longiflorum*, the Easter Lily, which also flowers quickly from seed and both have large, long and very fragrant white trumpet flowers. Other species worth growing are *L. auratum*, the fragrant Golden-rayed Lily and its varieties; *L. candidum*, the fragrant Madonna Lily; *L. speciosum* and its varieties with dots and splashes and shades of pink to crimson as well as the unusual *L. nepalense* var. *robustum* which has beautiful green flowers with a purple centre and is scented too. Of the hybrids 'Enchantment' with brilliant red flowers is especially recommended, as is the group to which it belongs – the Mid-Century Hybrids, all of which have upward facing flowers in shades of yellow, orange and red. Another good hybrid with outward facing flowers of pink and ivory, sometimes tinged very palely with green, is 'Corsage'. All these lilies will flower a few weeks earlier indoors than if grown in the open; the hybrids may be forced to flower earlier still but specially prepared bulbs are now available and these will flower in February–March.

When planting lilies the pots should first be half filled with compost; then a handful of sand should be sprinkled over it.

The bulb should be placed on the base and covered up to its head with compost, liberally mixed with sand. When the stem has grown above the rim of the pot further compost should be added up to an inch below the rim (i.e. the normal level for pot plants). The reason for this elaborate procedure is that the bulbs must be quite deeply planted to allow roots to form from the stems of the plants, while leaving them at the surface of the soil until growth is well under way reduces the likelihood of the bulbs rotting from excessive moisture. The exception to this rule is the Madonna Lily which should be planted shallowly with no more than an inch of compost over the bulb. As with other bulbs, the soil should be given an initial good soak, then be left with little or no watering until growth begins to show, when plenty of water should be given, but not overhead. The drainage must be good and an inch or so of gravel should be placed in the bottom of the pot.

The roots of the plants should be kept cool but the foliage needs plenty of sun, although the temperature should not go much above 20° (68°F).

Lilies are unfortunately very susceptible to several virus diseases and it essential to buy the bulbs from a reliable source. Do not be tempted by bargains. Fungal diseases will only occur if the humidity is too high and bulbs that are stored are also liable to the usual storage rot if they are not kept dry and well aired. Few pests attack lilies, the most usual being aphides.

Litchi

Litchi chinensis or *Nephelium litchi* is included for those who like to grow plants from pips because it can be grown from the lychee stone. Without bottom heat it may take a couple of months to germinate.

The plant is tender and unlikely to flower when young. Although it has quite attractive evergreen leaves it would otherwise hardly justify attention, except in a conservatory with plenty of room and a warm, humid atmosphere.

171

173

171. *Leucocoryne ixioides odorata*

172. *Lilium × testaceum*

173. *Litchi chinensis*

172

Lithops – see under MESEMBRYANTHEMUM

Lobivia – see CACTI

Lotus

Lotus bertholetii, the Coral Gem, makes an attractive plant for a hanging basket with its long stems of shellfish-claw-shaped scarlet flowers.

It has, however, a dormant period during the winter when the foliage tends to die back.

Luculia

Shrubs or small trees that will eventually grow large but nonetheless produce their intensely fragrant flowers when young – at least *Luculia gratissima* will – and in the winter. The flowers of *L. gratissima* are pale pinkish-white, in clusters. *L. pinceana* has larger, paler flowers and may also flower in winter. *L. grandifolia* has much larger leaves as the name denotes and beautiful, large fragrant white flowers. It is an outstanding shrub. Unfortunately luculias are deciduous or only partially evergreen.

Seeds are a surer method of propagation than cuttings.

Lycoris

A small genus of the Amaryllidaceae which should be cultivated like *Nerine* (q.v.). *Lycoris* flowers in late summer or autumn and needs plenty of sun to bring it into bloom.

Perhaps the most rewarding species is *L. squamigera* which has rose-lilac, fragrant flowers. *L. aurea*, with golden-yellow flowers, is also recommended.

Lygodium – see FERNS

174

176

174. *Lotus bertholetii*

175. *Luculia grandifolia*

176. *Lycoris squamigera*

175

Malpighia

Malpighia coccigera is a neat little shrub with leaves like holly and clusters of ingeniously shaped pinkish flowers over a long season. *M. punicifolia* is a much larger shrub, rather like a pomegranate, with leaves that are smooth above and bristly beneath; the rose-coloured flowers are followed by cherry-like edible fruit. Malpighias are evergreen.

They like the soil to be kept on the acid side.

Mammillaria – see CACTI

Mandevilla

Mandevilla laxa (syn. *M. suaveolens*), the Chilean Jasmine, is the most usually found species in this genus. It is a deciduous climber with beautiful, large, white, jasmine-like, fragrant flowers.

It should be planted in as large a pot as possible and then not disturbed. It can be cut back after flowering.

The young leaves are very susceptible to red spider mite and other pests; in fact, *Mandevilla* is one of the most pest-prone plants that an indoor-plant grower is likely to encounter and it is wise to spray them with a general insecticide once every two to three weeks because they are almost bound to have some pest or other at work on them. Those intrepid enough to try their hands with these difficult plants are warned against likely failure.

M. splendens has larger, rosy-crimson flowers and may be easier to grow in pots than *M. laxa*.

Manettia

Quite attractive evergreen climbing plants with small but profuse funnel-shaped flowers that may be red, orange or yellow. They are easy to grow and may flower throughout the year. They should be trained against a trellis or on strings or wire in a sunny window. Pruning during the course of growth will help them to flower well. Young plants do best and cuttings should be taken from the old plants in the spring.

177. *Malphighia coccigera*

178. *Malpighia glabra*

179. *Mandevilla splendens*

180. *Manettia inflata*

177

178

179

180

Maranta

Marantas, sometimes called Prayer Plants because the leaves of some species have the habit of folding at night, are much admired for their foliage. The smooth, oblong leaves have, in the most popular species, striking irregular markings, in the form of light green central blotches on a soft, velvety dark green background framed by purple veins as in *Maranta bicolor*, or with white veins and maroon blotches on a light green background as in *M. leuconeura*. The underside of the leaves is often purple. The plants have insignificant, small white or pink flowers in a raceme. Those most usually offered for sale are the varieties *kerchoveana* and *massangeana* of *M. leuconeura*.

Marantas need conditions as close as possible to those of the wet tropics. They must have a lot of warmth, water and syringing when in growth but should be kept on the dry side during the winter. They should be shaded or their leaves will curl and lose their colours. They should be re-potted in the spring when they can easily be propagated by dividing the roots.

Marantas are often confused with calatheas (q.v.) and other similar genera belonging to the Marantaceae. Among these are *Ctenanthe* and *Stromanthe*. *Ctenanthe oppenheimiana* is quite sturdy; its long dark green leathery leaves are marked with pale bands and are purple beneath. *Stromanthe sanguinea* has long shining dark green leaves which, again, are purple beneath, and attractive pink flowers. Plants of both these genera should be treated like marantas and calatheas.

Masdevallia *obrieniana* – see ORCHIDS

Medinilla

Medinilla magnifica is the Rolls-Royce of house plants. Although it does not grow very tall – about three feet – it has large magnolia-shaped, evergreen leaves and rather obscene, pendulous trusses of rose-pink flowers with purple anthers. The inflorescences, bearing several trusses, may be a foot or more long and are also long-lasting. Forms with deeper coloured flowers are also known.

Medinillas need the usual rainy tropical conditions of warmth, humidity and light; they should be frequently syringed. Plants may be pruned after flowering. They may be kept in the same size pot for many years but the soil should be renewed from time to time.

The Royal Horticultural Society's *Dictionary of Gardening* recommends that: 'Potting should be moderately firm to ensure short-jointed growth and the firm wood which is a necessity for successful flowering.' Given the right conditions medinillas, despite their exotic appearance, will flower readily.

Red spider mite is a likely pest.

181. *Maranta leuconeura* var. *kerchoveana*

182. *Medinilla magnifica*

181

182

Mesembryanthemum

The best known genus in the Aizoaceae. A fair number of these gaily coloured desert succulents can be grown outside in mild areas. There are others however that need protection at least from frost.

They make delightful house plants and are fun for children to watch emerge into life, but they must have a lot of light, sun and air. Some species develop woody stems and become small shrubs, others grow only leaves with flowers at the base or on stems while a few appear egg-shaped, like *Mesembryanthemum rhopalophyllum*, the growth dividing for the flower to emerge. The colours of the flowers may be yellow, white, pink, red or purple.

Mesembryanthemums need a rest period after growth is finished; they will usually sprout into growth again without the aid of water. Drainage for the plants must be good or they will rot at the base (particularly the stemless ones). They are, like all succulents, a prey to mealy bug.

Some other members of the Aizoaceae with similar characteristics are *Argyroderma*, *Cheiridopsis*, *Conophytum*, *Faucaria*, *Lithops* and *Pleiospilos*.

Miltonia – see ORCHIDS

Mimosa

What is frequently referred to as mimosa is in fact *Acacia* (q.v.). Mimosas have feathery leaves like those of acacias and feathery, rose to purple flowers which are unscented.

Mimosa pudica, the Humble Plant, is easily raised from seed and is usually grown as an annual though it is in fact a herba-

ceous perennial. Its leaves are very sensitive and quickly close up on being disturbed. It grows to about a foot high while *M. sensitiva*, the Sensitive Plant, is a partially climbing shrub which will reach three to seven feet. It is an evergreen and despite its name less sensitive than the Humble Plant.

Monstera

Monstera pertusa is a climbing plant that has large, shiny dark green leaves with, as the epithet denotes, deep serrations and holes in them. It is therefore a striking foliage plant that looks at its best when among a group of plants or else when incorporated into the design of the room so that the strange shapes of the leaves are shown off. It lends itself to easy imitation by plastic plant manufacturers. The cultivar 'Borsigiana' is a slightly more compact form. *M. deliciosa* has even larger leaves, similarly formed, but is too big for most people to cope with. (*M. pertusa* is often sold as *M. deliciosa*.)

Monsteras will sprout aerial roots that should not be removed but should be trained into the pot or a surrounding dish. The plants are fairly slow-growing and, although they come from the tropics, they appear to need less water and humidity than other foliage plants of similar origin. They are tough but the tips of the leaves may turn yellow from over- or under-watering.

Propagation is best done by layering of top shoots with roots.

183. *Mesembryanthemum criniflorum*

184. *Mimosa sensitiva*

185. *Monstera pertusa* 'Borsigiana'

183

184

185

Muehlenbeckia

The only plant in this genus to justify attention is *Muehlenbeckia platyclados* (syn. *Homocladium platycladum*), and that because it is curious rather than attractive. Young plants have flattened stems that look like leaves, from which the actual leaves project. As the stems grow older they become rounded. The 'flowers' are white, tiny and insignificant.

Musa*

It may seem slightly absurd to include a banana among house plants. We had not originally planned to do so but at the last moment we came upon an advertisement in the *New York Times* offering:

> tasty bananas year after year in your home ... a beautiful mass of wine-colored blooms this spring – followed by a succession of luscious, edible bananas. This amazing dwarf banana tree grows about five feet high; thrives inside your home so that delicious fruit is always within easy reach. Imagine, (*sic*) picking bananas for breakfast cereal, TV snacks. Use the surplus crop for banana cream pie, fritters, banana splits.

– All this from 'the Plantation Banana Tree'.

Hence this entry, although we have to confess to not yet having been able to obtain the plant to test its virtues.

Musa cavendishii is recommended (by the Royal Horticultural Society's *Dictionary of Gardening* and others) as the dwarf banana most likely to produce fruit in conservatory or even house conditions, but varieties of this species may be even better. *M. nana* and *M. velutina* are also recommended, by Ballard.*

M. cavendishii grows to some five feet tall and has two- to three-feet long bluish-green leaves. The yellowish-white flowers on a drooping spike are cupped in deep purple bracts: then, if you are lucky – or live in Florida – the flowers are followed by edible, fragrant bananas.

Plants flourish in conditions as close to those of their native South East Asia as possible, i.e. the rainy tropics. They need a lot of nutrient.

Taylor* warns against an insect pest, 'a black snout beetle whose grub-like larva bores in the corms'; if there is any sign of this the affected parts should be ruthlessly removed. The main disease to which *Musa* is prone is wilt and if this occurs the plant must be destroyed. There is a whole range of other exotic diseases that may occur, although they are unlikely to do so if the plants are carefully looked after.

* This entry is entirely drawn from secondary sources; in particular, George D. Ruehle in *Taylor's Encyclopaedia of Gardening*, Boston, 4th edition and the Royal Horticultural Society's *Dictionary of Gardening*, Oxford, 2nd edition, 1969. Also Ernesta Drinker Ballard: *Garden in Your House*, New York, revised edition 1971.

Muscari – see BULBS

Mutisia

Very attractive shrubs, usually climbing, with gazania-like flowers often brightly coloured.

Mutisia clematis, perhaps the most commonly cultivated species, is somewhat rampant and needs rigorous pruning in the spring to keep it under control. The flowers are bright orange-scarlet and, like those of other species, long-lasting. *M. decurrens* is outstanding, with magnificently large bright orange flowers. *M. oligodon* is also attractive.

186. *Muehlenbeckia platyclados*

187. *Musa nana*

188. *Mutisia oligodon*

186

187

188

Myrtus

Myrtus communis, the Common Myrtle, makes a delightful pot plant and deserves to be more widely known. The numerous small white flowers, a little like hawthorn, that appear in the summer are both attractive and fragrant, as are the dark glossy evergreen leaves which have to be rubbed to yield their scent. The variety, *tarentina*, has smaller leaves and is perhaps even more attractive.

Plants grow rapidly and can be pruned after flowering. To ensure that they keep their shape they should be turned periodically so that each part gets the same amount of light.

They are prone to attacks by mealy bug but are otherwise easy and trouble-free.

Naegelia – see SMITHIANTHA

Narcissus – see BULBS

Neanthe *elegans* – see *Collinia elegans*, under PALMS

Neomarica

A delightful member of the iris family, Iridaceae, that can be successfully cultivated as a house plant. The flowers of most species are yellowish with darker brownish bars but some species are multicoloured with blue, red, yellow brown and white.

Neomarica brachypus, flowers yellow, reddish-brown at base, with the disadvantage of having enormous leaves (up to six feet long in the natural state), and *N. gracilis*, white or tinted with blue, reddish at base, are recommended. The last species is viviparous and the plantlets may be rooted like those of *Chlorophytum*. All species are easily propagated by division of the rhizomes.

When growing and flowering the plants need a lot of water but they should be kept well drained.

189

189. *Myrtus*

190. *Neomarica caerulea*

190

Neoregelia

osmunda
+
No. 3

Neoregelias are bromeliads which are valued chiefly for their foliage because in general their flowers, tucked deeply into the leaf rosettes, are of little interest.

Neoregelia spectabilis is the most spectacular species, with crimson-tipped green leaves sometimes flecked with red on the upper surface while the underside is ash-grey and striped.

N. carolinae is a gaudy plant with yellow striped green leaves and deep red bracts at the centre of the rosette, surrounding the flower head: like *Cryptanthus* again, as if painted for a carnival.

Neoregelias like a higher temperature and more shade than other bromeliads but should otherwise be treated like *Aechmea* (q.v.).

Neoregelia used to be known as *Aregelia*, which is now considered incorrect.

Nepenthes

orchid or
sphagnum
mixture

Nepenthes, commonly known as Pitcher Plants, are curious and rather sinister plants, well worth cultivating for their strange habits and appearance, provided that wet tropical conditions can be adequately simulated.

The 'pitchers', which hang on slim tendrils from the tips of the long leaves, may be very large – three feet deep in one species but generally two to six inches – and they are usually coloured in combinations of green, red, purple or brown; the colour range has been further extended by the development of a number of hybrids.

Nepenthes are carnivorous plants and the pitchers are in fact insect traps, baited by nectar-secreting glands at their rim. Insects attracted to the nectar often topple in and slide down the slippery slope to the bottom of the pitcher where they come, literally, to a sticky end: a moveable 'leaflid', normally held partially open above the pitcher, closes down trapping them in the bowl of the pitcher where digestive and other juices break them down into food matter that the plant can absorb.

Nepenthes are mostly epiphytic and should therefore ideally be grown in hanging baskets or wall containers packed with an orchid mixture or two parts peat fibre mixed with sphagnum and a handful of charcoal.

If large pitchers are wanted shoots should be pinched out after several leaves have formed.

These are difficult plants and have been included because of their great curiosity. They should only be tried by those who can get very close to rainy tropical conditions. The plants should be shielded from direct sun and frequently syringed.

Seeds – obtainable in Britain and elsewhere – should be sown with bottom heat of 27–30° (80–86°F). They will nonetheless take upwards of a month to germinate.

Nephelium *litchi* – see LITCHI

Nephrolepsis – see FERNS

191

191. *Neoregelia marechalii*

192. *Nepenthes hookeriana*

192

Nerine

A strikingly beautiful autumn or early winter flowering member of the Amaryllidaceae. Suggested species are *Nerine bowdenii* (pale pink flowers), *N. flexuosa* (different shades of pink with white) which now includes *N. pulchella*, and *N. sarniensis*, the Guernsey Lily (scarlet, but variable). In addition there are the numerous hybrids of these species.

The bulbs should be bought and potted in August to September. They may either be potted singly in 4- or 5-inch pots or else three to four bulbs together in 6-inch pots, with the soil covering only half the bulbs. It is a help to add some dried cow manure or dried blood to the compost. They should then be treated like most amaryllids and lilies. That is to say, after the soil has had its initial watering, they should be left in a light place within a temperature range of 10–15° (50–59°F) until the shoots begin to appear, when watering should be re-started. From this point onwards, during the flowering season and throughout the winter, the soil should be kept moist but well drained. Then in May to June watering should be stopped and the plants allowed to dry out (the leaves of *N. flexuosa* will have already withered and yellowed). The bulbs should be kept in a dry but airy place until it is time to restart their active season again in August to September.

Nerines do not suffer from being pot-bound and should be left undisturbed in their pots for at least two seasons.

Nerium

Nerium oleander, the Oleander or Rose Bay, conjures up nostalgic thoughts of the Mediterranean where it is almost omnipresent.

The attractive, slim long evergreen leaves and the clusters of flowers in white, red, shades of pink or creamy yellow make it a lovely shrub to keep. Another species in this genus of three, *Nerium odorum*, is also cultivated but much more rarely than the Rose Bay. As its name denotes, it has the great advantage of fragrance. The leaves and flowers of all species are poisonous.

Neriums will respond well to plenty of sun and air. They can be stood outside during the summer. After flowering they should be cut back quite drastically to retain their shape and encourage new growth.

They are susceptible to scale insects, mealy bug and red spider mite.

Nertera

Nertera granadensis is a pleasing curiosity. It is known as the Bead Plant but might more appropriately be called the pincushion plant because the inconspicuous flowers are followed by bright, orange-red berries, like old-fashioned hat-pin heads, on a cushion of tiny, compact leaves.

Plants need abundant moisture when active but are otherwise undemanding and give little trouble. Any fragment of plant with roots will quickly prosper.

193

194

193. *Nerine sarniensis* var. *major*

194. *Nerium oleander*

195. *Nertera granadensis*

195

Nicolaia

Greenhouse plants rather than house plants but the usually brilliant orange-red clusters of bracts at the end of long flowering spikes are so spectacular that we could not resist including them to tempt those lucky enough to have the right conditions. They are members of the ginger family, Zingiberaceae.

To induce flowers the plants must be given plenty of fertilizer.

Nicolaia is the correct name for plants previously known as *Phaeomeria*.

Nidularium

osmunda
+
No. 3

Bromeliads, very similar to neoregelias (q.v.). *Nidularium innocentii* has brilliantly red inner 'bract-leaves' to its rosette and white or greenish sessile flowers; *N. fulgens*, perhaps the

most spectacular, has similar scarlet leaves to its rosette and violet flowers with white tubes enclosed in red sepals.

Nopalxochia – see CACTI

Notocactus – see CACTI

Ochna

A genus of some eighty or so species from Africa and tropical Asia. Among them, *Ochna serrulata* (or *O. multiflora*), a shrub from Natal, is of interest – primarily for the extraordinary and endearing form of the ripening fruits on the branches. At a certain stage these far more resemble winged insects – painted variants of a bumble bee conjured up by a child – than anything from the plant kingdom.

This arises from the irregular development of the fruits on the flower head. The yellowish-green petals quickly drop and the pink, deepening to cherry red, sepals are swept back as the small green berries begin to develop on a deep red rounded base. The sepals thus become the 'wings' of the imaginary insect. The five round fruits develop unevenly, often no more

than two or three at a time, and as they ripen and swell they darken, becoming the protruberant, shiny black 'eyes' of the insect. The picture is completed by one proboscis-like hair between the eyes and several other wispy 'antennae'.

A good plant will flower profusely and is a charming and unusual addition to the conservatory.

Ochnas require the standard treatment for tropical shrubs, but particular care should be taken to keep the soil well aerated. They are apt to produce slightly attenuated growth if the temperature is high and the light intensity low; in that case the tips of the branches should be nipped off.

196

198

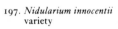

196. *Nicolaia magnifica*

197. *Nidularium innocentii*
variety

198. *Ochna atropurpurea*

197

Odontoglossum – see ORCHIDS

Oliveranthus *elegans* – see ECHEVERIA *harmsii*

Oplismenus

Oplismenus is a genus of mostly creeping grasses that look rather like tradescantias, especially those with variegated leaves, although the leaves are more elongated. *Oplismenus hirtellus* and *O. imbecillis* both have forms with variegated leaves.

They are quite tough plants and useful for hanging baskets or in foliage groups. They should be fed during the season of growth. The upper leaves of the younger plants are the more attractive and as cuttings root easily it is best to take them and thus keep up a supply of fresh plants. The flowers are of little interest.

Orchids

It can justly be claimed that the orchid family contains more wonderful flowers in colour, form and sometimes in fragrance than any other.

Rather surprisingly many orchids have a number of qualities that fit them admirably to be grown in the house, which is more than can be said of most of the popular flowering house plants such as cyclamens, azaleas (rhododendrons) or chrysanthemums. Their relatively limited cultivation may be due partly to the fact that they are thought to be rather expensive which, in the case, at least, of the commoner kinds is not true compared with many other indoor plants. More important, it is probably the exotic aura of orchids that has hindered them from becoming as generally popular as they deserve; they look as if they must be beyond the capacity of the amateur to cultivate successfully indoors.

However, provided that a few simple rules are observed – and certain basic rules have to be observed with all plants – quite a wide range of orchids can be brought into flower indoors more easily than most plants from the rainy tropics.

Orchids divide themselves naturally into three groups: those that are epiphytic or semi-epiphytic, i.e. those that live attached to another plant but whose roots derive their nourishment from the surrounding elements, not from the plant itself as does a parasite; those that are saphrophytic, i.e. that derive their nourishment from rotten vegetable matter (they are devoid of chlorophyll and have fleshy, much-branched rhizomes); and thirdly, conventionally terrestrial orchids.

The third group lives chiefly in temperate zones, is on the whole difficult to cultivate indoors and is omitted here; the small second group is so closely akin to the first that no separate comment is necessary.

Almost all the orchids, then, that can be grown successfully indoors are epiphytes or semi-epiphytes. They will usually attach themselves to trees in tropical forests and put out roots that will extract their growth needs from the atmosphere and mixture of dead and living growth surrounding them and from their association with fungi on the bark, often storing substances in pseudo-bulbs.

It will immediately be realised that conventional pot-plant treatment of an epiphytic orchid is far removed from its natural conditions of growth. These orchids are however very adaptable. It is, indeed, possible to simulate their natural conditions by enveloping the roots of the plant in a special mixture consisting basically of chopped osmunda fibre (the roots of certain osmunda ferns) and sphagnum moss with other substances added* and enclosing this in fine mesh netting in the shape of

---

* Sander, in his *Orchids and their Cultivation*, 7th edition, 1969, gives detailed recommendations for the main groups of orchid. The amateur, however, may confine himself to a cymbidium 'mix' and another more porous 'mix' for the truly epiphytic orchids. Both such 'mixes' are obtainable from a number of suppliers.

199. *Oplismenus hirtellus variegatus*

200. *Cymbidium* 'Vieux Rose'

201. *Dendrobium nobile* 'Virginale'

202. *Coelogyne ochracea*

199

200

201

202

a container. This method will only work satisfactorily if the atmosphere is very humid; otherwise the medium will quickly dry out. The plants can be – and more often are – grown in ordinary pots: the same compost mixtures should of course be used and particular attention must be paid to the aeration of the compost with chips, as well as to the drainage. Shredded chunks of fir bark are widely used in the U.S. for potting the epiphytic species.

This then is the first of the 'simple rules': the orchid roots *must* be well aerated and well drained, in the appropriate orchid compost.

The other 'rules' are merely those that apply to most flowering plants from the rainy tropics. The compost should be kept moist but not soaking. Precisely because orchid compost is – or should be – well aerated it will tend to dry out quicker than the medium used for other pot plants. More frequent attention is therefore necessary to ensure the right balance. Pots should never be left standing in water for more than an hour (they are usually best watered from the bottom and stood in the water, because the medium, being very porous, is unlikely otherwise to retain enough water); the only exception is in the case of certain orchids that have a dormant period when they should be kept almost wholly dry. Usually, the air should be as humid as possible to benefit both the roots and the leaves and make the flowers last longer, but the humidity requirements of many orchids are not exceptional.

Orchids like good ventilation but not draughts. They are quite moderate feeders and should have a general fertilizer no more than once every three waterings in the active season. Fish manure or its extract can have a dramatic effect on the size and number of flowers of cymbidiums and probably most other orchids.* They can also be given foliar nutrition. However, it is important not to over-fertilize orchids or the leaf growth will become too luxuriant at the expense of the rest of the plant and in extreme cases black markings may appear at the end of the leaves, where the excess nutrient has been forced.

The majority of orchids should have as much light as possible but should be protected from the direct rays of a powerful sun.

As to temperature, orchids are usually divided for convenience into three groups:

1. Cool. Those that will take a minimum of 10° (50°F) or in some cases less and should rise to 15° (59°F) or a little more in their most active season.

2. Intermediate. Those that should have a minimum of 15° (59°F) or a little less by night in the winter and that should have a temperature of 20–25° (68–77°F) by day during the active season.

3. Stove. A minimum of 20° (68°F) and a maximum rising to 30° (86°F) by day in the active season.

Those with which the indoor grower is most likely to be concerned are the intermediate group. They include a wide range of beautiful plants, from the magnificent *Angraecum sesquipedale* (Christmas Star), with large (up to six inches across) star-like white fragrant flowers which have foot-long spurs, or nectaries, to the minute *Masdevallia obrieniana* (Partridge in the Grass), with tiny speckled brownish green flowers, and they present no very difficult barrier to successful cultivation.

Moreover within these rules orchids, unlike so many other indoor flowering plants, are almost easy-going; for instance, because of their storage capacity they are not exacting about the precise moment of watering (a few days can be skipped without harm, particularly if the plant is not in flower. Some, such as cymbidiums, will even survive gross neglect.) Other advantages for the indoor plant grower are the long life of many flowers (over a month in a number of cases and often more), the smallness of many plants and the fact that some of them will flower in the winter.**

It is naturally best to start with orchids that are known to be particularly easy but even here there is almost an *embarras de richesse*. The most obvious area of choice is the large and magnificent range of cymbidium hybrids. These have been developed over the last seventy years or so from certain species, in particular *Cymbidium jansonii, C. eburneum, C. insigne* and *C. lowianum*. The result is a wealth of magnificent plants with long spikes of large flowers in a multiplicity of colours and shades, from the most striking combinations to pure pale yellows or pinks.

Some may find cymbidiums almost too overwhelming, in which case there are, for instance, dendrobiums and coelogynes with delicately graceful, often white flowers. Such are *Dendrobium kingianum* with sprays of small delightfully fragrant flowers suffused with rose, violet or purple and its equally lovely variety *album*, or else the ivory white, orange centred *D. infundibulum*; and coelogynes such as *Coelogyne cristata* and *C. ochracea* (this is fragrant); or the delicate *Odontoglossum rossii* (white with brown markings). Or, for contrast, there is the enchanting, miniature *Sophronitis coccinea* (syn. *S. grandiflora*) with smoky, orange-red flowers, the lovely *Vanda caerulea* with deep blue flowers (a very rare colour in orchids) or the exotic *Zygopetalum mackaii* and related species or varieties, usually very fragrant, with striking green petals blotched with brown and with purple and white lips.

Then there is a large group of paphiopedilums (Lady's Slipper Orchids, at one time known as cypripediums), cattleyas with numerous magnificent hybrids, and miltonias; and the list can go on.

The only particular care that orchids need, apart from the observance of the rules, is to keep them disease-free and to

---

* We are most grateful to Mr J. S. Pirie of Aquila Farm, Hamilton, Mass. for first calling our attention to this fact which has subsequently been well borne out.

** Some of the most reliable in this respect are *Coelogyne cristata, Dendrobium kingianum*, some paphiopedilums and most cymbidiums.

203. *Zygopetalum mackaii*

204. *Paphiopedilum* Sir Redvers Buller (left)
Millonia Angustine (right)

205. *Paphiopedilum* 'Alma Gaevert'

206. *Cattleya* 'Catherine Subod'

203

204

205

206

deal with their re-potting needs. Scale insects and red spider mites are apt to attack them; and some are unfortunately very prone to the tobacco virus, which is conveyed by tobacco smoke and destroys the veins of the leaves of cymbidiums.

Re-potting is complicated only in the sense that there is still controversy over the degree to which orchids should be pot-bound; 'should' in the sense of inducing better growth above the surface because there is no virtue in this unnatural condition. Cymbidiums, which are often grown very tightly potted, flower superbly when planted out. Certain dendrobiums, on the other hand, do seem to thrive when acutely pot-bound, although this may be a case of putting up with rather than enjoying that state. On the whole we feel happier not to see plants pot-bound.

When re-potting a plant all dead roots should be removed; they have a leathery consistency and are quite easily distinguished from the usually white, plump living roots and the

old compost should be well shaken out. This applies particularly to cymbidiums whose roots live only for about two years. They ought to be re-potted every second year but not necessarily in larger pots: it is never wise to over-pot a plant because the soil in which roots are inactive turns sour and most epiphytic orchids have scant roots.

Finally it must be stressed that only the general guide-lines have been given here. Orchids offer such a wealth of interest and enjoyment that it is well worth buying one or more of the excellent monographs on them in order to master the subject in detail.*

* e.g. John W. Blowers, *Orchids*, London, 1962. David Sander, *Orchids and their Cultivation*, London, 7th edition, 1969. Rebecca T. Northern, *Home Orchid Growing*, New York, revised edition, 1969. Harry B. Logan, *Orchids You Can Grow*, New York, 1971.

Osmanthus

Evergreen shrubs which when still small can make delightful house plants as they have an abundance of little white or creamy, usually fragrant flowers. Some species also have blue-black berries.

Osmanthus delavayi flowers in April; *O. fragrans* flowers later and is outstandingly fragrant; the variety *rotundifolius* of *O. heterophyllus* (syn. *O. ilicifolius*) is dwarf and flowers in late summer.

Oxalis

A large genus with several low-growing species which flower abundantly and take up little space. Many are hardy and can be grown outside, in fact do so all too often and become treated as weeds; but they are recommended here because they are pretty in both leaf and flower and flowering seasons of different species succeed each other throughout most of the year. The leaves are often in rosette form, rather like a many-'leaved' clover, and flowers may be red, yellow, white or lilac, often in an umbel.

Oxalis adenophylla has greyish green leaf rosettes and delicate lilac-pink and white flowers, in spring. *O. cernua*, often called

Bermuda Buttercup, has bright yellow flowers in spring, sometimes continuing throughout the summer; and *O. deppei* has red flowers from spring to summer. *O. enneaphylla* has large white, fragrant flowers, prettily tinged with green at the centre, from spring to early summer. *O. variabilis* is variable, having white or red flowers with yellowish tubes, from October to December.

Some of the species spread rapidly and so the plants need to be kept under good control. They have a dormant period when the flowers and leaves die and the plants should then be put aside in a cooler place and kept barely moist.

207

207. *Osmanthus delavayi*

208. *Oxalis adenophylla*

208

Pachystachys

Pachystachys lutea with its prominent spikes of yellow bracts, looks very superficially like *Aphelandra squarrosa* to which it is related, but its habit of growth is less rigid and it is altogether a much more graceful plant.

The small white, purple-tinted, flowers that emerge from the bracts are an attractive contrast but they do not last very long.

Plants demand the usual rainy tropical treatment.

Palms

Palms (at least in Britain) may still have an association with large public rooms in Edwardian hotels. But it would be good to be rid of any lingering prejudice on that score because most of them have a graceful symmetry that can contribute a lot to a room or a hall – quite apart from their agreeable evocation of blue skies and sun.

What is more, a large number of palms acclimatise themselves very well to the sort of indoor conditions that prevail in northerly countries. That is to say that they can survive hot, dry air as well as temperatures below 10° (50°F). They are also toughly resistant to pests and diseases.

They can be planted in a No. 3 compost or in one part loam, one part sharp sand, one part peat, with charcoal added to the crocks.

Their simple requirements are moderate watering throughout the year and rather acid soil; they appreciate periodic doses of sequestrene (iron chelate) and of potassium sulphate.

Although most palms will ultimately become very large many of them are slow growers in this context and therefore will not be too demanding of space.

Among the numerous genera and species to choose from the following may be mentioned: *Butia leiospatha*, dwarf, but leaves three feet long; *Chamaedorea glaucifolia* that will flower when less than three feet tall, *C. ernestii-augustii* (syn. *Elentheropetalum ernestii-augustii*) with large partially divided leaves, and *C. radicalis* – all three very graceful; *Chamaerops humilis* has beautiful complete fan-like leaves; *Collinia elegans* (syn. *Chamaedorea elegans*, *C. pulchella*, *Neanthe elegans*) a tree with a notched green stem; *Dictyosperma album* with very slender, graceful pinnate leaves; the phoenixes, particularly *Phoenix dactylifera*, the Date Palm, and *P. pusilla*; *Rhapis cochinchinensis*; *Syagrus weddeliana* (syn. *Cocos weddeliana*), a very graceful small plant with delicate, arched, pinnate leaves; *Trithrinax acanthocoma*, dwarf-stemmed; *Washingtonia filifera* with curious white thread hanging from edges of leaves.

The best method of propagation is by seed, which despite high bottom heat, will take some weeks to germinate.

Pandanus

A large genus of woody perennials with long, pointed leaves, looking somewhat like *Dracaena deremensis* except that the leaves are usually toothed along the edges and, beneath, along the midrib. They grow from the central axis in a spiral formation giving rise to the plant's common name, Screw-pine.

Pandanus veitchii has dark green, spiny leaves up to two feet long with silver or white borders. *P. lindenii* has even longer leaves with pale stripes. *P. graminifolius* and *P. pygmaeus* are the smallest species, growing to barely two feet high with leaves twelve to eighteen inches long.

Pandanus should be treated broadly like dracaenas (q.v.). It is important not to let water remain in the leaf axils during the dormant season because it may cause rot. During this period the plants should be kept on the dry side.

The plants multiply naturally by the formation of offsets, often from aerial roots; these can be detached and planted in separate pots.

210

209. *Pachystachys lutea*

210. *Palms* mixed:
     Dictyosperma furfuraceum (1)
     Chamaerops humilis (2)
     Phoenix loureirii (3)
     Phoenix lanceana (4)

211. *Pandanus veitchii*

209

211

Paphiopedilum – see ORCHIDS

Passiflora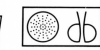

Passion Flowers are such rampant climbers that they are best suited to a conservatory where they will have plenty of room to expand. But the flowers are so spectacularly beautiful – the leaves and the fruit also are attractive – that it is impossible to exclude them for those lucky enough to have room. They can be cut back drastically to fit the space. In any case all superfluous tendrils should be removed because they twine round the flowers and spoil their shape.

As is well known, the plant gets its name from the resemblance to the instruments of the Crucifixion that early South American missionaries thought they detected in the parts of the central gynophore.

Passiflora caerulea appears to be the most popular species, with its white petals and blue, white and purple corona. But others of interest are the more fragrant *P. actinia* with white petals and a striking white, red and blue corona; *P. amethystina*

with bright blue petals and deep purple corona; *P. antioquiensis* with fine rose-red petals and violet corona; *P. racemosa* with lovely rosy-crimson sepals and petals and a purple, white and red corona. Then there is *P. quadrangularis* which both has large beautiful flowers (pinkish-white petals and a blue purplish-red and white corona) and delicious fruit, given enough light and warmth to ripen it.

Passifloras should not be planted in soil that is too rich or they may produce a super-abundance of foliage and no flowers; they must have plenty of light.

They most probably will be attacked periodically by mealy bugs and if so should be treated immediately for the bugs can cause great damage.

New plants are easily propagated by layering as well as by seed.

Pelargonium

Pelargoniums, commonly though erroneously referred to as geraniums, have fallen from the height of their Victorian popularity, partly no doubt because of the inevitable reaction to over-exposure and partly because of their association with flower beds in public gardens. They are however delightfully attractive and often showy plants whose different species and hybrids offer a great variety of size, shape and colour. Many of them flower for months on end and some have beautifully scented leaves.

Pelargoniums fall into three main groups: the Zonal pelargoniums (including the 'fancy-leaved', variegated types), Regal pelargoniums and Ivy-leaved pelargoniums. In addition there are the Scented-leaved varieties whose flowers are not usually very impressive but whose intoxicating scent more than makes up for this and the Miniatures, or 'Angels', which provide a delicate and colourful display for those without space for the full-sized plants.

The distinguishing feature of the zonal group, *Pelargonium × hortorum*, is a darker, roughly horse-shoe shaped zone of colour running across the leaves. They flower almost continuously throughout the year with no marked period of dormancy. Red is the dominant colour and single rather than double flowers are the rule, although double forms have been developed and colours may range from white through pink, orange, scarlet and crimson to magenta, the flowers often having white eyes

or darker veins; the magenta-flowered forms usually flower earlier than the scarlet. Several species are believed to have played a part in producing *P. × hortorum*, including *P. inquinans* and *P. zonale*.

They are very easy plants to grow and deserve a return to favour.

The regal group, *P. × domesticum*, is a hybrid group in which the plants are more shrubby than the erect, thick stemmed zonal group. Their leaves are darker in colour, unzoned, and often hairy, but the main difference is in the flowers, which are larger, more showy and often double. Their predominant colour is mauve, often blotched, streaked or striped in a darker tone. A disadvantage is that regal pelargoniums are dormant in winter: they flower in early summer.

The ivy-leaved pelargoniums are probably crosses between *P. peltatum* and other species. They have fewer flowers on each head and are closer in colour to the regals than the zonals – ranging from subtle shades of lavender and mauve through pink, cerise, salmon and scarlet. They will flower throughout the summer and may continue during the winter, too, if given enough light. The ivy-leaved pelargoniums are more straggling in habit than the others and therefore particularly suitable for hanging baskets.

212. *Passiflora caerulea*

213. *Pelargonium × hortorum* 'Gazelle'

214. *Pelargonium × domesticum* 'Carisbrooke'

215. *Pelargonium peltatum* 'L'Elegante'

Cuttings of all pelargoniums (except the miniatures which are generally more tender in every way) are easily taken. The shoots should be strong with at least three to four nodes and be cut off cleanly just below the lowest node; then the lowest leaves should be removed, leaving only the one or two nearest the top. The cuttings should be inserted into a mixture of sand and peat, with or without loam. No fertilizer is needed at this stage. When rooted they should be transferred to a No. 3 compost for growing on. Cuttings for summer-flowering plants are best taken in September and for the winter-flowering zonals in March/April. In the latter case any flower-buds that form before October should be nipped off: this should be done in any case until a good plant has developed. After flowering pelargoniums may be pruned heavily – to within five inches of the ground for small compact plants.

Pelargoniums like plenty of light and unpolluted air at an average temperature of 15° (59°F). They are unfortunately subject to a number of diseases of which blackleg – a softening of the base of the stems due primarily to too much moisture – is the most lethal. They must therefore be only sparsely watered and very well drained. They can in fact stand quite long periods of dryness. Plants should be watched for white fly and aphis.

Pellionia

Primarily a foliage plant of which the two most worthwhile species are creepers: *Pellionia repens* (syn. *P. daveauana*) and *P. pulchra*. The former has dark bronzy-green, oval leaves slightly tinged with violet. The latter, a more attractive plant, has dark green leaves and veins with splashes of silver at the centre; it has small greenish flowers in umbels.

Pellionias need wet tropical conditions: a temperature not below 15° (59°F) and plenty of moisture. They like the shade.

For illustration see with *Dichorisandra*, plate 98.

Peperomia

A genus of small, succulent or near succulent, plants that are valued primarily for their foliage although in some species the inflorescence, in the form of a spike or a catkin, adds greatly to the appearance and interest. *Peperomia caperata*, in particular, has dramatic fleshy white spikes that branch at the ends and contrast strikingly with the background of crinkly dark green leaves. Equally striking are the wavy white rat's tails that emanate from the smooth, thick-leaved *P. obtusifolia* (of which there is a form 'Variegata' whose leaves have irregular splashes of green on a yellow background). Then there are *P. argyreia* (syn. *sandersii*) which has thick silvery white leaves tapering to a point with dark green radiating out from the veins and *P. hederaefolia* which by contrast has rather dingy grey-green quilted leaves (though the veins are a darker green) and really can only justify itself as part of a grouping of plants. A number of peperomias have a trailing habit which makes them suitable for hanging baskets and there is also the climber, *P. scandens*, rather similar to *Philodendron scandens*, which has a variegated form.

Peperomias are almost epiphytic and need little soil. They should be watered very carefully from below and must have plenty of time to absorb all they need – although they should not stand permanently in water. It is best therefore to allow the plant almost to dry out before watering, then stand it in water for about half an hour, and tip away any that remains.

Persea

The only species in this genus of interest to the house plant grower is *Persea gratissima* (syn. *Persea americana*) – the Avocado Pear – and the reason for including this is not because it has any outstanding qualities but because it is fun to grow from the stone.

If you plant the stone in a pot with the pointed end upwards a stalky tree will soon be produced, with a canopy of elliptical green leaves which are all too apt to turn brown at the edges if the roots are allowed to become too dry. In its natural habitat the tree will grow up to sixty feet but in the house it should be stopped by pinching out the top bud at about eight inches high, when it may branch. It will not, alas, produce fruit when kept as a house plant.

Phaeomeria – see NICOLAIA

Pharbitis – see IPOMOEA

 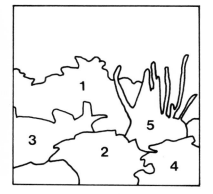

216. *Peperomia* mixed:
    P. argyreia (1)
    P. caperata (2)
    P. obtusifolia variegata (3)
    P. marmorata (4)
    P. sandersonii (5)

217. *Persea gratissima*

217

216

Philodendron

The charm, coupled with the relative toughness of several species, has won the philodendron justified eminence among climbing foliage plants; there are also attractive shrubby species.

For convenience philodendrons may be divided into two groups. On the one hand are those with entire, heart- or arrow-shaped leaves of which *Philodendron scandens* (sometimes called *P. cordatum*) may be taken as the prototype. It is very hardy and although it will respond to care with full, smooth, dark green leaves and vigorous growth it will survive a degree of neglect and remain static with rather limp, forlorn leaves. It will put out aerial roots from the leaf nodes and should therefore ideally have a surface lined with sphagnum to which it can attach itself.

In this group also comes *P. melanochrysum* which is the juvenile form of *P. andreanum*; it has larger, dark green, conspicuously pale veined leaves that appear to glow with an iridescence in an appropriate light. Then there are *P. eru-*

bescens with large arrow-shaped leaves, pinkish when young, becoming dark green with a wonderful natural sheen; *P. ilsemanni*, leaves variegated; *P. wendlandii* with long lance-shaped leaves (this species is not a climber); and many others.

The prototype of the second group may be taken as *P. bipinnatifidum*, which has large deeply incised leaves similar to a monstera. In this group come *P. elegans*, with more delicate leaves, that is quite robust and *P. laciniatum* – both climbers; and a number of others including the hybrid *P. × rubris nervis* with dark shining green leaves and red veins.

We have said that some species of philodendron are quite hardy but it must be remembered that they all come from tropical South America and therefore thrive best in similar conditions. All will respond to and some demand a high temperature, a high degree of humidity and plenty of light.

Stem cuttings with three joints or top shoots of old plants root easily with bottom heat.

Phoenix – see PALMS

Phyllanthus *nivosus* – see BREYNIA

Pilea

The only species in this rather undistinguished genus that is worth attention is *Pilea cadierei* with attractive dark green, pointed, leaves splashed with silver. The shoots should be quite ruthlessly stopped to obtain a compact, bushy plant. *P. microphylla* (syn. *P. muscosa*) is little more than a curiosity that will discharge a cloud of pollen if shaken when the insignificant

flowers are out; hence its common names: Artillery Plant, Gunpowder Plant, Pistol Plant.

Pileas are tough and usually trouble-free. Plants should be fed regularly to maintain the leaf colour.

218

218. *Pilea cadierei* 'Nana'

219. *Philodendron scandens*

219

Piper

This genus contains *Piper nigrum*, Black Pepper, but the only species at present of interest as a house plant is the climbing *P. ornatum*, with rather large heart-shaped bright green leaves, splashed with pink along the veins.

Although it will tolerate shade, the colouring of the leaves will be more vivid when there is plenty of light. Great care must be taken to ensure that the temperature does not fall below 15° (59°F), otherwise the leaves will drop and the plant may die. The plant likes moisture and as it produces roots at the leaf nodes it will do well when trained up a surface wrapped with sphagnum moss.

Pittosporum

Quite a large genus of evergreen shrubs or trees, a number of which come from Australia and New Zealand. These pittosporums make appealing house plants because of the delightful fragrance given off by their small flowers, often in clusters, during the winter.

Pittosporum bicolor, *P. cornifolium* (musk-scented), and *P. patulum*, all with flowers in various shades of red; and *P. eugenioides*, with yellow flowers, are recommended but there are several others well worth having.

Platycerium – see FERNS

Pleiospilos – see under MESEMBRYANTHEMUM

Plumbago

Plumbago auriculata (syn. *P. capensis*) only just qualifies for inclusion in this book because its habits of growth are untidy and it is better off stood outside during the summer (from June to October) than it is if kept indoors as it delights in plenty of full sun and only needs protection from the cold.

However the beauty of its pale blue phlox-like flowers, which come in abundance from June to November, is such that it has been included for the benefit of those who cannot enjoy it in the garden. It is admirably suited to a largish conservatory. It is an easy plant for indoors as it is quite happy with dry air, demanding only plenty of light – and warmth with ample watering during the active season. There is a variety, *alba*, whose white flowers do not have the beauty of the blue.

P. auriculata is a fast grower and quickly becomes straggly but can be cut back at will. Some plants soar upwards but others tend to spread their branches and can be used in hanging baskets.

If plants are to be stood out in the summer this must not be done too early because the unhardened leaves will be damaged and die, which is unsightly. Under some conditions *P. auriculata* is semi-deciduous in that most of the old leaves die during the winter simultaneously with the growth of new ones. The dead leaves should be carefully removed from the plants.

P. auriculata may be propagated by rooted shoots from the base of the plant or by almost ripe cuttings.

P. rosea is a tall shrub with similar flowers that are deep crimson pink. Again, we do not feel that this touches the beauty of the pure blue *auriculata* but it has the advantage of flowering in winter. It needs more warmth than *P. auriculata* and should not be stood outside during the summer.

220

222

221

223

220. *Piper ornatum*

221. *Pittosporum crassifolium*

222. *Plumbago auriculata*

223. *Polyscias balfouriana* with *Vriesia simplex*

Polypodium – see FERNS

Polyscias

Some of these shrubs (or trees) have a mysterious attraction; and for many people, to judge from the sale of 'Ming Trees' in New York and elsewhere.

As 'foliage plants' they have not the formal elegance of a *Dracaena marginata* or a *Schefflera actinophylla*; nor have they the beauty of leaf of many others. Yet they have a strange appeal. They come from the islands of the South Pacific and South East Asia and as young plants usually have fairly straight, regular, pale stems or trunks although with the distinctive, notch-like lenticels; subsequently they may be-come greatly distorted and roam all over the place: part of their attraction. From the stems will emerge, in the case of *Polyscias balfouriana* or *P. paniculata*, tufts of short-stalked leaves or in the case of *P. filicifolia* with quite long stalks.

These plants provide dramatic decoration to a large, modern room or give variety to a group.

As their habitat indicates, they demand conditions similar to those of the rainy tropics.

Primula

A very large and delightful genus of over five hundred, chiefly alpine, species from the North Temperate zone of which only some are suitable as house plants. Those that are have great advantages because they need neither a lot of light nor a lot of heat and they appeal to the true 'gardener's' instinct because they are best grown from seed. They should be treated as annuals.

The species most suitable as house plants are *Primula malacoides* with large flowers ranging in colour from carmine to lilac and white, *P. obconica* in many shades of colour such as carmine, mauve, blue or white, and *P. sinensis*, also having a wide range of colour from bright scarlet through mauve to white. One of the purest and most heartening spring flowers (although it is rather taller and also later than other species) is the chance hybrid, *P. × kewensis* which has beautifully scented, bright yellow flowers.

Seeds should be sown at the end of May or, in the case of *P. malacoides*, in late June or early July, for flowering in the following late winter/early spring; sowing can of course be staggered so as to have a longer succession of flowers. A special Seed-sowing or a similar compost should be used. They are best sown in boxes or pots outside, covered with glass until they germinate. They are prone to damp off and should be watered with Cheshunt Compound (2 parts copper sulphate, 11 parts ammonium carbonate, diluted 1 oz to 2 gallons of water) or a similar fungicide at the time of sowing. The plants should be thinned out as soon as possible and transferred to individual pots (or several to a large pot). A No. 3 compost should be used. They like quite a lot of moisture and a cool, airy atmosphere and they should be shaded from direct sun. They must be brought in before there is any danger of frost and kept in a coolish temperature of about 10° (50°F), though *P. obconica* likes it a little warmer.

Primulas are unfortunately liable to a variety of fungus diseases that cause rot or leaf spotting. In the former case treat with Cheshunt Compound and in the latter take off the leaves and destroy them. They may also become victims of certain virus diseases which cause stunting and yellowing of the leaves. Immediately such symptoms are seen the infected plant must be destroyed. Vine weevil may attack them and gamma-BHC is the best remedy.

One warning: primulas are known to cause dermatitis in some people and those with sensitive skins should wear gloves when handling them.

Prostanthera

A genus of attractive shrubs from Australia that are often delightfully scented in flower, leaf, or both – commonly known as Australian Mint. The delicate sprays of smallish, usually bell-shaped flowers in shades of violet-blue, mauve, pink or white are quite profuse and, moreover, appear at the end of winter or early spring when there is relatively little else.

Prostanthera lasianthos, P. ovalifolia, P. rotundifolia and *P. sieberi* are some of the best species.

Some plants will profit from quite heavy pruning, as they are apt to become rather spindly.

Pseuderanthemum

A genus of graceful flowering shrubs. *Pseuderanthemum malaccense* has long terminal spikes of delicate lavender flowers faintly freckled with red, and those of *P. tuberculatum*, equally delicate, are white and single. Both flower abundantly.

P. malaccense should be discarded after one season; cuttings can be taken any time from March to June for flowering the next year and should be well pinched back to encourage a good shape.

224

224. *Primula malacoides*

225. *Primula obconica*, mixed

226. *Primula × kewensis*

227. *Prostanthera ovalifolia*

228. *Pseuderanthemum tuberculatum*

225

226

227

228

Pteris – see FERNS

Punica

Punica granatum, the Pomegranate, particularly its dwarf form *nana*, makes an attractive house plant. Its light green, rather delicate-looking foliage, its bright orange-red flowers and, from time to time, even, its pomegranate fruit have much appeal over a long season. It is inclined to shed its leaves in winter although if given enough light and if not allowed to dry out it may keep them.

The shoots, particularly if the plant has been cut back to maintain its shape, are liable to be too abundant for the plant's appearance or performance and should be thinned out in the spring.

Rebutia – see CACTI

Rechsteineria

A useful member of the Gesneriaceae that is tuberous (tubers of older plants will grow very large, up to a foot or more) and can be cultivated in the same way as gloxinias (see *Sinningia speciosa*). The flowers are usually in bright shades of red.

Rechsteineria cardinalis, with flowers rather similar in shape and colour to those of *Salvia splendens* can be induced to flower almost all the year round if dead flower stems are consistently removed; otherwise it will have a few months'

dormancy. *R. leucotricha*, another attractive species, has flowers in softer tones of pink or salmon.

The leaves of the plants are liable to scorch if exposed to direct, hot sun.

Rechsteinerias are often crossed with sinningias and there are some worthwhile hybrids.

Rehmannia

A small genus of perennial plants from China and Japan with exotic, trumpet-shaped flowers.

Rehmannia angulata is a compact plant with reddish-purple flowers with yellow spots in the lower part of their throats. *R. glutinosa* is also compact, with yellowish-buff and purple flowers. *R. elata* which is a larger plant whose flowers have

purplish lips with a yellow throat spotted with red, should be treated as a biennial. There are some ten species and a few hybrids have been raised.

They are not difficult and seem not to mind quite a cool, dry atmosphere.

229

229. *Punica granatum nana*

230. *Rechsteineria cardinalis*

231. *Rehmannia glutinosa*

230

231

Reinwardtia

There are two species in this genus: *Reinwardtia indica* (syn. *R. trigyna*) and *R. cicanoba* (syn. *R. tetragyna*). They are both well worth cultivating for the clusters of quite large, single yellow flowers produced in winter.

The young plants need to be pinched back often to make them bushy. They ought also to be exposed to plenty of sun and air so that they ripen well.

Cuttings of nearly ripe growth with the head pinched out, will take easily.

Rhapis – see PALMS

Rhipsalidopsis – see CACTI

Rhododendron

The genus *Rhododendron* includes azaleas which are only one of the many series the genus is divided into. The original distinction of the azalea as deciduous and the rhododendron as evergreen no longer holds good. It is an immense genus and many species are suitable for indoor cultivation.

In appearance the shrubs usually have dark or grey-green leaves, sometimes with a shiny, sometimes with a more or less woolly upper surface, the larger being oval and tapered, the smaller often rounded. The flowers are usually bell- or funnel-shaped, in clusters and have a wide range in size; they are usually abundant, sometimes scented, and their colour generally runs from white through many shades of yellow, pink, salmon and mauve to deep red.

Rhododendron simsii is the source of many delightful hybrids and those of *R. edgworthii* are fragrant. Hybridisation of *R. ciliatum* has also produced some lovely scented plants, such as 'Countess of Haddington' (× *dalhousiae*) and 'Princess Alice' (× *edgeworthii*). Then there is the outstanding 'Fragrantissimum' a cross between *edgeworthii* and *formosum*. Among the fragrant species *R. maddenii*, with large white flowers often touched with rose, is particularly worth noting; as is the superb *R. lindleyi*, with pure white flowers. Among the early forcing rhododendrons (azaleas) for November and Christmas, Rochford recommends the Petrick varieties for white or pink, *ambrosiana*, bright red, and 'Princess Beatrix', salmon.

In the U.S. there is a rather different range from which to choose and each coast has its species, varieties and hybrids that do best in that area.

Chiefly from ignorance many people have found a beautiful plant in the midst of flowering wilt within twenty-four hours of its arrival, shedding flowers, buds and leaves. They naturally conclude that these plants are 'difficult'. This need not be so if a few basic rules are followed although it must be realised that rhododendrons flourish naturally in the reverse of usual household conditions. Many of those rhododendrons sold as house plants must be partially shaded, although several of the less usual species need good light to flower well; they must have the right soil, be kept moist though well drained and even a little aerated; the atmosphere should not be simultaneously hot and dry.

If the pots are allowed to dry out the plants will wilt immediately and the emergency action of immersing them for five minutes in a basin of warm water should be taken. Pots are apt to dry out quickly because of the composition of the soil. To counteract the harmful effect of dry artificial heat the pots should be kept in a bowl of constantly moist pebbles or peat. Rochford and Gorer* give some very useful advice on how to gauge whether a plant has the right degree of moisture: the waterline on the main trunk should be constantly watched; the perfect condition is for the waterline – easily identified as a clearcut ring above which the trunk is dry – to be half an

* Rochford and Gorer, *The Rochford Book of Flowering Pot Plants*.

232

234

235

236

232. *Reinwardtia indica*

233. *Rhododendron christianae*

234. *Rhododendron dalhousiae*

235. *Rhododendron maddenii*

236. *Rhododendron veitchianum*

233

inch above the surface of the soil. If the waterline is further up the trunk the soil must be allowed quickly to dry somewhat or rot will set in and the leaves will begin to drop. If – and this is more likely – the waterline is below the half inch mark or invisible, the plant is too dry and should be watered. One must use common sense in looking for the waterline: if the soil is evidently very moist the waterline may be quite high, even in the lower branches, but if the plant is dry and there is no sign of a waterline the conclusion is obvious.

Rhododendrons need no soil fertilizer apart from a periodic sprinkling of peat to retain the soil's acidity and the addition when potting on – best done every other year – of charcoal to keep it 'sweet'. However they do benefit from foliar feeds: various proprietary brands are available and, as usual, instructions must be carefully followed.

When the plants are in bud before their main flowering, any side shoots that spring out should be nipped off, so that the plant's energies are concentrated solely on the budding and flowering processes. Even then, the flower buds of some of the more difficult species or hybrids such as *R. edgworthii*, *R.* 'Fragrantissimum', and *R. lindleyi* may shrivel if the conditions are wrong.

Rhododendrons growing outdoors are subject to quite a wide range of diseases and pests, but indoors they are usually trouble-free although they may be affected by gall, shown by swellings on the leaves or stems. This is not particularly harmful and the stems affected may be allowed to remain if the alternative is destruction or mutilation of the plant. Other pests are the azalea leaf miner, the rhododendron bug, leaf hopper, red spider mite and white fly; and there are more too. Spraying with malathion is currently the best remedy.

Some of the small-leafed rhododendrons can be fairly easily raised from cuttings (under glass, over heat) but the large leafed ones should be grown from seed or layered.

Rhoeo

In a contest for oddity of appearance among the plant kingdom *Rhoeo discolor* would come high. Although this plant belongs to the trandescantia family, the stiff pointed leaves radiate from a central stem like a member of the Bromeliaceae; they are dark green, tinged with deep purple underneath. From the leaf axils protrude slightly open 'mouths' that have been compared with purses or boats and inside them are tiny white flowers. The variety, *vittatum*, gives a rather gaudy impression with cream stripes on the upper side of its leaves.

Plants should not be given much water in the winter.

Offsets are readily created by year-old plants.

Rhoicissus

Rhoicissus rhomboidea is a vigorous evergreen vine, similar in its requirements to *Cissus antarctica* to which it is related, and perhaps even more hardy. It is useful as a trellised room divider or to enliven a dark corner, as it requires little light and tolerates gas or other fumes. The cultivar, 'Jubilee', with larger, slightly leathery leaves, is slower-growing and sometimes preferred for that reason.

An undemanding plant, but water sparingly in winter.

Rochea

Rochea coccinea, the most usual species in this small genus related to *Crassula*, puts forth terminal clusters of scarlet or carmine, scented flowers from its rather leathery-leafed, twelve-inch stems.

Plants are easy to grow and well worth cultivating for their scent alone. After flowering, the stems should be cut back to some six inches from the soil to encourage side shoots.

237

237. *Rhoeo discolor*

238. *Rhoicissus rhomboidea*

239. *Rochea coccinea*

238

239

Ruellia

Quite attractive plants both for their large flowers, usually in various shades of deep red as in *Ruellia graecizans* (syn. *R. amoena*), pink or mauve, which will often appear in winter, and, in some species for their foliage such as *R. devosiana*, with white tinged pink flowers.

Plants need a high degree of humidity or they will not flourish and their leaves will curl.

Saintpaulia

The enchanting African Violet, *Saintpaulia ionantha*, is deservedly one of the most popular house plants. Growers have produced many variants but the original species with the simple purity of its single violet-blue flowers and conspicuous yellow stamens is hard to excel; and to us a bit pointless also because where nature has attained such perfection why compete? Growers have however great achievements to their credit in producing varieties that will hold their flowers for longer than usual.

Aside from the violet-blue flowered varieties, there are shades of white, pink and reddish-mauve, both single and double, available. When choosing a plant go for strong healthy-looking dark green leaves and plenty of buds. The plants that you buy are likely to be in a highly fertilized mixture in order to produce quicker growth and more abundant flowers, and you should be sparing with fertilizer during the first few months.

It would be wrong to suggest that saintpaulias are easy to cultivate. It is true that anyone with even a tinge of green to their fingers can keep a healthy shop-bought plant in flower for some two months. But although saintpaulias flower almost continuously in their natural habitat or in a warm greenhouse they will have two or three periods of dormancy in a normal house. It is at the first dormancy period that the owner must show his skill, or it will also be the last.

Like all flowering plants from the rainy tropics saintpaulias need a humid atmosphere and quite a high temperature – between 20° and 25° (68° and 77°F) during the day – in order to thrive. Assuming that the temperature is 20–25°, the day-time humidity should be at least 50%. In fact at no time should the humidity percentage be allowed to drop below 50% for long. To achieve this it is wise to keep the pot immersed in damp peat, or in a bowl on a layer of pebbles with water up to the bottom of the pot. Saintpaulias must also have good light although they should be shaded from direct sun which will damage the leaves and the flowers. These requirements apply just as much when the plant is not in flower as when it is. If this were more borne in mind there would be fewer pathetic little plants, unlikely ever to flower again, sitting around neglected or forgotten in unused corners of so many houses. Saintpaulias do not have a rampant root system and can therefore be kept successfully and economically in tiny pots by professional growers. Amateurs will lessen the need for constant attention and therefore probably have more success if they transfer the plants to larger pots after the initial burst of flowering is over.

Saintpaulias can be propagated by seed (difficult for the average house plant owner), by leaf cuttings (considerably easier) or – and this is the most practical method for amateurs – by the division of plants. If you use that method, wait until the plant has temporarily ceased to flower and cut it down the middle with a sharp knife, dust the cuts with sulphur powder or some other fungicide and leave the two sections to dry for about twelve hours, then plant them in separate pots and ensure that they have impeccable conditions as described above. Saintpaulias may in fact often reproduce themselves naturally by sending out offshoots that quickly reach a similar size to the parent plant: this makes the task of division easier, although there will still be an element of severance and therefore dusting to prevent rot remains essential.

The hazard to which even well-tended saintpaulias are prone is rot, which may come from over-watering or from allowing rot to spread from a dead flower or leaf. But plants may be attacked by mealy bug, tarsonemid mites or other insects and a constant watch should be kept on them (as on all other plants).

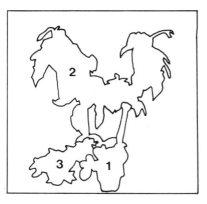

241

240. *Ruellia* mixed:
    R. formosa (1)
    R. graecizans (2)
    R. prostrata (3)

241. *Saintpaulia ionantha*

240

Sansevieria

In some people sansevierias arouse feelings of intense distaste. Elbert and Hyams, for instance, write: 'This is about the lowest level to which the lily family sinks. We detest them for their appearance . . .' We do not know why they should have been singled out for such hostility as they seem to us to have more positive qualities than a number of foliage house plants (they look more cactus- than lily-like).

Although the flowers are unappealing the long, sharp-pointed leaves of *Sansevieria trifasciata* have a dramatic quality when the plants are set either among a group of succulents or against a uniform background. For those who like variegated foliage, this species has a variety *laurentii* with creamy yellow longitudinal stripes.

Particular care should be taken not to over-water plants during their dormant period.

Saxifraga

A large, varied genus of rock plants, most of which are hardy and of little interest to the house plant enthusiast.

Saxifraga stolonifera, however, (syn. *S. sarmentosa, S. chinensis*) is a useful small plant for mixed groupings, particularly in hanging baskets or stands when the fringe of fine runners with plantlets developing at their tips is an attractive feature. The plant's common names are Mother of Thousands, Roving Sailor, Strawberry Geranium.

S. stolonifera has pretty, rounded leaves, laced with a delicate tracery of paler veins on the upper side and tinged with red beneath. The variety *tricolor* is, as its name implies, truly variegated green/cream/red – but it is much more tender. Both forms have tall panicles of small white star-like flowers, each with two tiny pink dots at their centre.

S. stolonifera is a very easy to plant to grow; it is almost hardy but needs good light to flower well (May to June) and to bring out the red tinge on the undersides of the leaves. Water moderately throughout spring and summer and keep only just moist in winter. Propagation is simply a matter of pinning down plantlets in suitable soil and cutting them off the parent runners when rooted. (*S. stolonifera tricolor* does not always root easily.)

Green fly is the worst pest.

Schefflera

A genus of numerous species of shrubs or trees, one of which, *Schefflera actinophylla*, is gaining popularity as a house plant because of its elegant, stalked, smooth, elongated oval, dark green leaves; another species, *S. digitata* (syn. *Aralia schefflera*) has toothed edges to its leaves.

These species will grow very large in favourable conditions but young plants, or larger ones if room can be found, make an attractive addition to a group of differently shaped foliage plants, or they will stand out well against, say, a clear, white background.

Plants are not demanding in their requirements.

242. *Sansevieria trifasciata laurentii*

243. *Saxifraga stolonifera*

244. *Saxifraga cymbalaria* var. *Huteana*

245. *Schlefflera digitata*

242

243

244

245

Schizanthus

One of the many outdoor annuals that are now being rediscovered as a source of indoor pleasure much earlier in the year.

Schizanthus has been called Poor Man's Orchid and Butterfly Flower for the shape and delicacy of its flowers, which may be in a wide range of colours, from deep carmine through pink and violet to cream and white, usually with a yellow centre. The leaves are equally delicate, a lacy pale green mantle to the plant, which may be about eighteen inches high in all.

Schizanthus pinnatus is the most usual species, and has been crossed with *S. grahamii* to produce *S. × wisetonensis* which has excellent compact forms for indoor cultivation. The large 'Pansy Flowered' or 'Improved Danbury Park' schizanthus is another attractive form.

Schizanthus seeds should be sown in August, in a cool greenhouse or frame (in fact anywhere frost-free – no extra heat is needed for germination which is generally excellent). The seedlings should be transferred into 3-inch pots and potted on frequently until the plants have reached the desired size. (This is very important and if not done as soon as the root tips touch the sides of the pot, growth will slow up and the plant begin to flower prematurely. Regular inspection of the soil ball is the only answer.) Then a little more warmth, gradually up to about 20° (68°F), will soon encourage them into flower. They are showy plants and will flower profusely from about February to April. Water more generously during the flowering period.

The main problem with schizanthus is to prevent the young plants from shooting up too quickly and becoming 'leggy' – a tendency which is best curbed by keeping them fairly cool until the flower buds appear. In any case they will need good staking.

Other hazards are root rot, stem rot, powdery mildew and leaf gall. These are all easily cured but should be watched for. Otherwise schizanthuses are easy plants to grow and provide a lightness and variety of flower at a time when not much else is available.

Schlumbergera – see CACTI

Scilla – see BULBS

Scindapsus

The cultivated species of *Scindapsus* are climbing plants with heart-shaped leaves, rather like *Philodendron scandens*. Unsupported, in hanging baskets for instance, they also trail gracefully.

Scindapsus aureus has irregular yellow markings on its leaves; *S. pictus* has light green markings on a dark green background and the variety, *argyraeus* (which is in fact a juvenile form of *S. pictus*), has its leaves spotted with silver.

The spathe-sheathed spadix of flowers is unappealing and will only be produced by the more mature plants.

Aerial roots are thrown out and the easiest method of propagation is to cut off a piece of stem with roots attached and pot it up.

246. *Scindapsus aureus* 'Silver Queen'

247. *Schizanthus pinnatus*

246

247

Sedum

Most sedums are hardy and suitable for the border or rock garden and some people may see little point in importing them into the house. There are however some tender species that combine well with other members of the family, Crassulaceae, such as echeverias and sempervivums and with cacti.

The leaves are usually fleshy and the numerous flowers pink or yellow. Some sedums die back in winter and are therefore best avoided. *Sedum acre* (Stonecrop) and *S.*

spathulifolium, both hardy, are attractive plants with a mass of yellow flowers; *S. sieboldii* has pink flowers and, particularly in its variegated form *mediovariegatum*, is one of the tender species that is popular as a house plant.

Propagation is very easy – in fact *S. acre* can quickly become a rampant weed when not confined to a pot, as each leaf broken off and allowed, purposely or accidentally, to remain in contact with the soil may root and form a new plant.

Selaginella

A very large genus of moss-like plants of which a number of species make quite an attractive addition to a group of ferns or foliage plants. The genus ranges from hardy to stove plants and some species are trailing in habit.

There are numerous worthwhile species, among which *Selaginella bakeriana*, *S. denticulata*, *S. kraussiana* (all trailing),

S. caulescens and *S. lepidophylla* (a curiosity) are perhaps the most interesting.

Plants should have plenty of water but the soil medium should be very light and well drained. In general, they should be treated like ferns.

Sempervivum

A hardy genus of the Crassulaceae which will group well with other members of the family such as echeverias, kalanchoes and sedums.

Most sempervivums form a series of rosettes close to the ground and from these arise the flowering stems with numer-

ous white, yellow, red or purplish flowers. *Sempervivum arachnoideum* with rose-red flowers and cobweb covered leaves is one of the most rewarding.

The easiest method of propagation is by detaching young plantlets arising from the older plants.

Senecio

Senecio is a large genus belonging to the Compositae or Daisy family as do chrysanthemums and euryops etc. (q.v.). It ranges from *S. vulgaris*, the common groundsel, through exotic shrubs like *S. heritieri* whose flowers are violet-scented with rosy-crimson and white petals and a purple central 'disk'. Some senecios such as *S. heritieri*, *S. hectorii* and *S. kirkii*, the last two with white daisy-like flowers, are attractive plants for the conservatory but too large for most houses.

We might not have felt justified in including *Senecio* were it not that *S. cruentus* is the source of the whole range of hybrids known as 'Cineraria'*.

Cinerarias flower so abundantly and the many colours make such a brilliant display that they are popular pot plants even though they should be treated as annuals and despite their over-use in business window-boxes and corporation gardens.

If you are put off by the lurid blues and maroons, search out the more subtle deep brownish-red shades. The hybrida multiflora nana race, growing to about one foot, is well suited to house plant conditions. The hybrida grandiflora race has particularly beautiful large flowers and grows about two feet high.

Cinerarias need a cool, moist atmosphere with plenty of light but shading from direct, hot, sun.

If you have a glass frame or cool greenhouse cinerarias are easy to raise from seed. For winter flowering sow very thinly in April in pans of light sandy compost and cover lightly. Either pot off singly into thumb pots or prick out in boxes, then transfer to 3-inch pots.

Cinerarias are a paradise for white fly – but they are also susceptible to damage from a number of substances used in insecticides and care should be taken to avoid these.

* It seems that Cineraria has now been abandoned as a true genus.

248. *Sedum acre*

249. *Selaginella* mixed: *S. apoda* (left)
     S. kraussiana (right)

250. *Sempervivum arachnoideum*

251. *Cineraria multiflora*

248

249

250

251

Setcreasea

A small genus of, usually, creeping plants somewhat similar to tradescantias or zebrinas, to which they are related.

Setcreasea striata has dark green leaves with ivory-coloured veins. *S. purpurea* may be more erect and has purple-coloured leaves; it will produce curious purple and white flowers on a tall stem, cupped by large purple bracts. *S. purpurea* is a fast grower.

For illustration, see with *Asparagus*, plate 22.

Sinningia

Sinningia speciosa is the species from which the florist's Gloxinia has been developed. The grandeur of the trumpet-shaped blooms in a rich variety of stained-glass colours – white and shades of red, blue and purple or these colours edged with white as well as more exotic colour-combinations – have made the plants deservedly popular.

They can be grown from seed, in which case they need a temperature of at least 20° (68°F) to germinate; from tubers when they can be started five degrees (nine degrees Fahrenheit) lower, although they are happier with a high temperature; or, quite easily, from stem or leaf cuttings.

The seeds, which are tiny, should be sown in early February. They should be given only a very light covering of soil and watered with Cheshunt Compound or a similar preparation to prevent damping off. They should be shaded until they sprout. When the seedlings are large enough to handle easily they should be pricked out, either several to a pot and later transferred singly to 6-inch pots, or they can be planted directly in individual pots. Tubers should be planted in individual pots with their tops protruding very slightly from the compost to lessen the risk of rot attacking them. Once the plants are in full growth they should have plenty of water. They need good light although they should be shielded from strong direct sun. The leaves are brittle and also mark easily; thus tap water should not be allowed on them; rainwater should be used for syringing if at all possible.

The greatest danger to *S. speciosa* is rot developing in the tubers as a result of too much moisture. A particular form of this is foot rot which blackens the base of the plant's stem. Watering with Cheshunt Compound (2 parts copper sulphate, 11 parts ammonium carbonate, diluted 1 oz to 2 gallons of water) is a good preventive and the condition can be cured by the application of sulphur powder.

After the plants have flowered the leaves will begin to die back, at which point watering should cease. The tubers can either be stored in the soil in their pots or, if this is not convenient, they can be carefully removed from the dry soil for storage; in either case they should not be put in a place where the temperature drops below 10° (50°F) or they may be damaged. The tubers are best re-started in early February to flower in mid-summer, or up to a couple of months thereafter for later flowering.

Other species of *Sinningia* are somewhat overshadowed by the development of *S. speciosa* but the small *S. concinna* and *S. pusilla* and their hybrids are well worth cultivating as they will flower all the year round, provided that they have enough warmth, light and moisture. Lastly, *S. tubiflora*, an erect-stemmed plant, growing to three feet high or more, should be mentioned because of its scented elegant white or cream flowers; it must have plenty of light but, like other sinningias, should be protected from the direct rays of the full sun; it is best to stake it carefully to prevent the rampant flower stems getting out of shape or breaking.

Apart from rot the other chief hazard is mealy bug which may well establish itself close to the base of the plant.

Smithiantha

Smithiantha, formerly known as *Naegelia*, is a very useful member of the Gesneriaceae because it can be induced to flower in profusion throughout the winter. Like the achimenes it has scaly rhizomes but the flowers are tubular and bell-shaped without the flattening of *Achimenes longiflora*.

Interest is now mainly concentrated on the hybrids, particularly those developed at Cornell University and by Butcher's of Surrey, England. These are more compact plants than the species and their flowers range over a diversity of colours.

Culture is as for *Achimenes* (q.v.) except that the rhizomes are very active and need to be planted only one to a 5-inch pot; further, the soil in the pot needs to be kept just moist during the period of dormancy, otherwise the rhizomes may die off.

The easiest method of propagation is by division of the scaly rhizomes.

252. *Sinningia speciosa*

253. *Smithiantha* hybrid

252

253

Solanum

Solanum capsicastrum, the Christmas Cherry, is the small shrubby plant covered in round green, yellow and red berries (various stages of ripeness) that appears in shops and city window-boxes with monotonous inevitability every autumn. Some varieties have oval berries, and there is a variegated form. *S. pseudocapsicum* is a larger species, slightly later fruiting, and its variety *weatherilii* has mainly orange, oval, pointed berries.

Solanums need light to colour the berries but they should be shielded from any very hot sunlight to prevent the berries ripening and falling too quickly. This indeed, is the main problem, and Elbert & Hyams recommend a pinch of Epsom salts added to the water every three weeks to help retain the berries.

Plants are best grown as annuals from seed and summered outdoors.

Spotted wilt, potato blight (*Solanum* is a member of the potato family), foot rot, grey mould, dropsy, stem canker, green fly, thrips and red spider may attack.

Soleirolia

Soleirolia soleirolii (previously known as *Helxine soleirolii*), the solitary member of this genus, is a rapidly growing, creeping plant with small, round shiny leaves. It is quite a useful plant for a group and will stand both cold and shade.

Sollya

A small genus of delightful Australian twining shrubs with brilliant blue small pendent flowers. The common name of *Sollya fusiformis* (or *S. heterophylla*), the Bluebell Creeper, is descriptive of the flowers. *S. parviflora* is on a lesser scale but does not lack a gentle charm.

Young shoots are liable to become infested with green fly.

Sonerila

Sonerilas are valued primarily for their decorative foliage although *Sonerila speciosa* has quite striking mauve flowers. The leaves of *S. margaritacea* are covered on the upper side with pearly-white spots and there are several varieties of this plant with differingly marked leaves.

Bright sun will damage the leaves, causing them to shrivel.

Sophronitis – see ORCHIDS

254. *Solanum capsicastrum*

255. *Soleirolia soleirolii*

256. *Sollya fusiformis*

257. *Sonerila margaritacea*

254

255

256

257

Sparmannia

A small genus of shrubs or small trees belonging to the Lime family. *Sparmannia africana*, African Hemp, is the species usually found. Its graceful, soft, large, pale green leaves and its delicate, scented white flowers with puffs of purple-tipped filaments make it an attractive, unusual plant to seek out.

It must have plenty of light and air but is otherwise not very difficult: it can survive quite low temperatures or a dry atmosphere.

Plants grow with disconcerting speed but can be cut back sharply after flowering. They may be attacked by red spider mite.

Spartocytisus *nubigens* – see CYTISUS

Spathiphyllum

A genus of the arum family: plants whose true flowers are borne on a spadix enclosed by a spathe (large bract – in this case *phyllum*, leaflike).

Spathiphyllum wallisii is the species most usually available and the shiny lanceolate leaves with slightly wavy edges make a graceful foil for the long-lasting 'flowers'. The spathe is at first pale green, the it gradually turns white, so giving rise to the common name White Sails, and finally green again as the seeds on the spadix ripen. The main flowering period is spring but there is often a second, autumn flowering. *S.* × 'Mauna Loa' is larger and scented but a more delicate plant.

S. wallisii is a moisture- and shade-loving plant but it does like a certain amount of warmth and plenty of food. It grows quickly and needs repotting about once a year – preferably early spring before the flowers develop: plants may be propagated at this time by division.

Red spider is the spathiphyllum's worst enemy but a humid atmosphere, which the plant prefers, should deter it.

Sprekelia

Sprekelia formosissima, the Jacobean Lily, is the sole, out-standingly graceful species in this genus. The solitary flower, on a long stalk, may be crimson or white; there are also several varieties.

The bulbs should be treated in the same way as hippeastrums (q.v.). They should be only one-third covered with soil to which a sprinkling of dried blood has been added and the drainage should be good. After they have been well watered in they should be kept on the dry side until there are signs of growth when they should be given plenty of water until the leaves begin to die off (this may not happen under humid conditions). As with hippeastrums the period of growth after flowering is important for the next year's success. If the bulbs can be started with a bottom heat of 20–25° (68–77°F) results will be quicker and more certain.

Like similar bulbous plants, they are prone to mealy bug at the leaf bases.

258. *Sparmannia africana*

259. *Spathiphyllum* ×
    'Mauna Loa'

260. *Sprekelia formosissima*

258

259

260

Stapelia

A number of species will appeal to those with a sense of the macabre. *Stapelia variegata* is the scion of the genus; the squat starfish-shaped flowers, usually brown or yellow, mottled with one or other of these colours or with black, on leathery stems, look like lower marine or animal life feeding off putrescent vegetable matter. To complete the picture, the flowers have a curious sticky centre (of pollen) and initially give off a slight odour of rotting meat or fish which attracts flies to lay their eggs in them. The flowers of several other species smell disgusting.

Stapelias are succulent plants and need to be well watered and very well drained during their active period but to be kept almost wholly dry in winter because they have a propensity to rot.

As is usual with succulents the chief pests are mealy bugs on the leaves and at the roots.

Stenocarpus

A genus of evergreen trees and shrubs from Australia, of which *Stenocarpus sinuatus* is the most suitable as a house plant. In its natural habitat it may grow up to a hundred feet high but young plants are attractive additions to the house or conservatory and can be kept to manageable proportions by judicious pruning.

The plant is generally cultivated for its decorative foliage alone (in the usual form – there is another, oval leafed form not worth growing indoors); the leaves are large, deeply divided, and tinged with red when young, maturing into a warm yellow-green. However this species does flower when young and *if* full light can be given it will produce clusters of fine, brilliant red flowers.

Stenocarpus likes a lot of light, but apart from that it is a very easy plant to grow, requiring a minimum temperature only a few degrees above freezing (*S. salignus* and *S. sinuatus* are hardy in the Scilly Isles).

Stephanotis

For those who value highly the scent of a flower *Stephanotis floribunda* (Madagascar Jasmine), ranks with *Citrus*, *Gardenia* and Jasmine among the most cherished of house plants: its glossy dark green leaves are elegant and it can be induced without great difficulty to put forth numerous clusters of scented, graceful, waxy white flowers (rather like a very large jasmine). They will also produce large smooth oblong green fruit, turning to yellowy-brown. Fortunately plants are now quite freely available from the shops.

You must, however, ensure that the plant has plenty of light and a daytime temperature of 20–25° (68–77°F) during the flowering season in the summer or you will not get good results. Sometimes disappointments are caused by lack of humidity: all the promise of a newly acquired, fully budded plant in the peak of condition may evaporate as the buds gradually yellow and shrivel due to lack of moisture in their new atmosphere. It is important to be aware of this danger with new plants and to take every possible step to avoid it (see Introduction, p. 7). Once well established the plants are quite rampant climbers and you will doubtless need to cut them back drastically from time to time. This can be done without danger in the spring; in fact such pruning seems to induce more abundant flower buds. It is best to dab a little cigarette ash or suchlike on to the cut stems to stop bleeding.

Mealy bugs unfortunately feast on these plants and so they must be watched carefully and sprayed at the first signs.

Stem cuttings of the previous year's wood, taken during pruning in the spring, should be planted singly in pots and placed in a propagating frame. They need a steady temperature of at least 25° (77°F) and high humidity.

261

261. *Stapelia variegata*

262. *Stenocarpus sinuatus*

263. *Stephanotis floribunda*

262

263

Strelitzia

Strelitzias have such striking flowers that they have been included although one has to have a lot of room (plants eventually grow up to five or six feet high) to be able to cope with them. They will not flower until they are mature but the bluish-green leaves of *Strelitzia reginae*, the most usually cultivated species, shaped like those of a banana plant (it belongs to the same family), are themselves handsome. They have a pronounced pale midrib, sometimes tinged with pink in young leaves, later white.

Plants need plenty of water, humidity and sun in the summer but should be kept rather dry during the winter. The base of the plant grows big quite rapidly and so re-potting should be carried out at least every two years – in March before growth re-starts. The need for re-potting will become apparent through the roots forcing the base of the plant above the level of the soil and themselves becoming partly visible like stilts. At this point the opportunity can be taken to obtain additional plants by division of the roots.

Streptocarpus

One of the easiest and most rewarding of the Gesneriaceae. A number of the species are worth cultivating and there are some beautiful hybrids, deriving chiefly from *Streptocarpus rexii*. The original species have flowers that are usually shades of blue or else white but hybrids from *S. dunnii* with brick-red flowers have considerably widened the range of colours; the clear, soft blue 'Constant Nymph' is nonetheless still the most outstanding.

With careful management the flowering season of these plants can be extended over several months. There will be a tendency for them to die back in the winter but new leaves will soon start to sprout on most plants provided that watering is carefully regulated.

Plants can be raised from seed sown any time from February to April in a minimum temperature of 15° (59°F). Existing stock can be increased by leaf cuttings, which are easily made, or by division of larger plants.

Streptosolen

The solitary member of this genus, *Streptosolen jamesonii*, is a gaily attractive evergreen climber with abundant clusters of bright orange and yellow flowers from about June onwards until winter.

By ruthless pruning the plant can be turned from a climber into a smallish bush, or else it can be allowed to trail freely from a hanging basket.

Strobilanthes

A large, variable genus, some species of which are very attractive and not difficult to cultivate. Most species have flowers in shades of blue or purple.

Strobilanthes dyerianus is an outstandingly pretty plant with pale blue flowers and large, pointed, dark green leaves with rose-purple patches at the centre. Young plants look best and are often grown for the foliage alone. *S. isophyllus* is a much smaller plant whose attraction is in the flowers rather than its nettle-like foliage.

Stromanthe – see under MARANTA

264. *Strelitzia reginae*

265. *Streptocarpus hybridus* 'Constant Nymph'.
See also plate 138 with *Gesneria*.

266. *Streptosolen jamesonii*

267. *Strobilanthes isophyllus*

268. *Strobilanthes dyerianus*

264

265

266

267

268

Syagrus – see PALMS

Tetrastigma

A robust, large-leafed vine, closely related to *Cissus*. It is quite tough and well worth growing but needs a large-scale setting to do it justice. *Tetrastigma voinierianum* (syn. *Vitis voinieriana*) is the most usual species in cultivation and its young leaves are densely clothed in hairs, rather like light green velvet.

Thunbergia

The genus *Thunbergia* contains some striking shrubs and climbers.

Thunbergia alata, Black-eyed Susan, the species most usually seen, is a climbing annual that is hardy enough to grow outside and therefore scarcely comes within the scope of this book. Among the more tender perennials *T. grandiflora* is a magnificent climber with large mauve-blue flowers, but it needs a lot of room. *T. laurifolia* is similar, with smaller leaves; *T. fragrans* is scented as the specific epithet denotes; *T. erecta* is a non-climbing shrub which bears numerous, pendent, deep blue flowers with orange throats and yellow tubes; it should be pruned after flowering. There are other species well worth growing if they can be come by.

Tibouchina

One of the loveliest shrubs that will flourish indoors. The handsome leaves of '*Tibouchina semidecandra*'* are strongly veined and have a downy surface and the beautiful, large, deep purple flowers have a velvety sheen.

T. semidecandra (or *T. urvilleana*) is naturally a large shrub, inclined to become leggy and lose its lower leaves but, after flowering in autumn/winter, it can take heavy pruning – down to the last shoots of the young wood.

We have found plants to be rather easily damaged by certain aerosol insecticides or greenhouse defumigants. Tibouchinas are not usually prone to pests and so should be moved to safety when insecticides are to be used.

Cuttings of half-ripe shoots may be taken at any time and grown, preferably in a propagator, at about 20° (68°F).

* It appears that the true *T. semidecandra* is not in cultivation and the species usually offered under that name is in fact *T. urvilleana*. Roy Hay and Patrick M. Synge, *The Dictionary of Garden Plants in Colour, with House and Greenhouse Plants*, London and New York, 1969, p. 365.

Tillandsia

osmunda

Among the most exotic bromeliads with extraordinary inflorescences, better seen in the species illustrated than described (a daunting feat).

Tillandsia lindeniana which has attractive leaves as well as spectacular flowers is perhaps the finest species. *T. cyanea* is also very fine and there a number of other interesting species. The flowers of *T. lindeniana* and others come out one at a time in succession up the stem. They are the truly exquisite element of the plant but are, alas, shortlived (although there are many of them). The bracts however retain their colour for several weeks.

Do not allow the soil to be saturated with water and there is no need to syringe in winter. For general instructions, particularly how to induce flowers, see *Aechmea*.

269

269. *Tetrastigma voinierianum*

270. *Thunbergia erecta*

271. *Thunbergia grandiflora*

272. *Tibouchina semidecandra*

273. *Tillandsia cyanea*

270

271

272

273

Tolmiea

The one species in this genus, *Tolmiea menziesii*, is notable chiefly for its habit of forming new plantlets on the old leaves. These can be trained into a jar of water or moist soil and children can watch the plantlets develop.

The large toothed, heart-shaped leaves and their stalks are hairy.

The plant is very easy, tolerating a low temperature and poor light. It should always be kept moist.

Trachelium

Perennial herbs from Mediterranean countries. *Trachelium caeruleum* grows to a height of two to four feet and has large corymbs of small, scented blue flowers; *T. lanceolatum*, a much smaller plant, less than a foot tall, has flowers of a very similar shade and *T. rumelianum* (syn. *Diosphaera rumeliana*),

a sprawling plant, has lilac-coloured flowers.

Seeds should be sown in February in gentle heat for flowering the same year, or cuttings can be taken in spring or autumn.

Trachelospermum

A genus of climbing shrubs with white or pale yellow flowers that are in general delightfully scented.

Trachelospermum jasminoides is perhaps the best species and has clusters of white flowers with a beautifully strong fragrance. *T. asiaticum*, with creamy coloured flowers, is also

strongly scented.

Plants can be cut back as much as desired after flowering.

The young shoots are liable to attack by white fly and red spider mite.

Tradescantia

Some species of *Tradescantia*, above all *Tradescantia virginiana*, are hardy herbaceous perennials and do not concern us here. The more tender species are grown primarily for their varieties with variegated foliage, such as those of *T. fluminensis*, and are remarkably resilient. The species most usually found have a creeping or trailing habit and are good additions to mixed foliage hanging baskets.

Plants can be pinched back to keep a good shape but when they show signs of ungainliness or of going off it is best to take cuttings, which root easily.

If any part of a variegated variety shows signs of reverting to the plain green foliage of the type it should immediately be removed.

Trichocereus – see CACTI

Trithrinax – see PALMS

274. *Tolmiea menziesii*

275. *Trachelium caeruleum*

276. *Trachelospermum jasminoides*

277. *Tradescantia fluminensis vittata aurea*

274

275

276

277

Tulbaghia

A genus of rhizomatous plants with umbels of attractively graceful flowers, violet in the case of *Tulbaghia pulchella*, *T. fragrans* and *T. violacea*; white (and fragrant) in the case of *T. natalensis*. The leaves of many species have a scent of garlic.

Plants have a short dormant period in the winter when watering should be reduced.

Tulip – see BULBS

Vallota

A handsome South African bulb which may take a little while to get established but, once it has become so, will flower beautifully. *Vallota speciosa* (syn. *V. purpurea*), the Scarborough Lily, has bright scarlet flowers but there are varieties or cultivars in white or various shades of pink and red.

Bulbs should be treated like *Nerine* (q.v.) except that they should be planted, preferably, from March to July; they should then flower in late summer or early autumn. Water sparingly at first but liberally when the bulb is in growth; never allow to dry out completely. Vallotas are best left undisturbed for two to three years before re-potting. After the first year they will need periodic feeding when in growth – but over-feeding will generate too luxuriant foliage and side-bulbs at the expense of flowers.

Vanda – see ORCHIDS

Veltheimia

Quite attractive bulbous plants from South Africa with racemes of numerous tubular flowers which in the case of *Veltheimia capensis* are pale pink tinged with green and of *V. viridifolia* are a darker pink spotted with pale yellow. (In fact the plant usually sold as *V. capensis* is likely to be *V. viridifolia*.) The crinkly edged, shiny leaves are also handsome.

Bulbs should be treated like *Hippeastrum* (q.v.). If planted in August to September they will flower in the winter.

Veltheimias should be given plenty of water when in growth but after flowering should be kept on the dry side when some, though not all, of the leaves will die back.

Vitis *voinieriana* – see TETRASTIGMA

278. *Tulbaghia violacea*

279. *Vallota speciosa*

280. *Veltheimia capensis*

279

278

280

Vriesia

Spectacular epiphytic bromeliads closely related to *Tillandsia* (q.v.) from which they differ by having ligules on the petals. On the whole vriesias have more ornamental leaves and less striking flowers, although it is hard to equal *Vriesia splendens* which fully justifies its name. As with tillandsias the flowers (yellow in this case) are shortlived but the bright red bracts will retain their colour for some eight weeks.

For general instructions see *Aechmea*.

Washingtonia – see PALMS

Yucca

A genus of trees and shrubs similar to agaves or dracaenas, with a number of species that have ornamental value as house or conservatory plants. Most are hardy up to *c*. latitude 50°.

On the whole the stemless or short-stemmed species and hybrids are best for indoors; *Yucca aloifolia*, *Y. whipplei*, *Y. glauca* and *Y. gloriosa* may be mentioned. The flowers, usually white or creamy-white, possibly tinged with purple and sometimes scented, are borne on erect or pendent panicles. A number of species will not flower until they are several years old and it is worth checking this when buying plants.

Yuccas are in general very tough but they nonetheless respond to care by producing better textured foliage and more numerous flowers. If possible, stand them outdoors during the summer.

Propagation should be by taking fleshy root cuttings, two to three inches long.

Yuccas may be attacked by a leaf spot that causes brown patches with black spots on them. The infected leaves should be cut out immediately and the plant sprayed with Bordeaux mixture or a similar preparation.

Zantedeschia

The genus is best known through the species *Zantedeschia aethiopica*, the Arum Lily or Lily of the Nile. The pure white flowers or, more exactly, the pure white spathe surrounding the creamy yellow spadix, is strikingly beautiful, rising from the shiny green foliage; and the scent is intoxicating. *Z. elliottiana* with its bright yellow spathes is almost equally striking, although unscented; *Z. melanoleuca* with pale yellow spathes and *Z. rehmannii*, dwarf, with pink spathes, are also worth growing.

Zantedeschias thrive in marshlands in South Africa and the closer that you can get to such conditions the more success you will have. They like a rich soil, plenty of water, light and warmth. The tubers should be planted in early autumn, one or more to a pot depending on the size of the pot, an inch below the surface of the soil and well watered in. Then they should be watered only very sparingly until they start to sprout, when watering should be stepped up; when they are well under way liquid fertilizer should be added. Because they are prone to rot at the base of the leaves it is advisable to water the plants from below.

Z. aethiopica will do well outside during the summer but *Z. elliotiana*, *Z. melanoleuca* and *Z. rhemannii* and tender and should be kept under glass.

The yellow species flower about a month later than the white.

Zantedeschias may be attacked by various forms of leaf, root or corm fungi. In the first case brown spots form on the leaves which should be destroyed. In the other cases, watering with Cheshunt Compound, Captan, or soaking in a 2% formalin solution when you re-pot the plants should cure them. There is also a virus disease, spotted wilt, whose symptoms are white spots or streaks on the leaves or stems as well as a distortion of the leaves. The infected plants have to be destroyed.

281. *Vriesia splendens*. See also with *Polyscias*, plate 223

282. *Yucca aloifolia*

283. *Zantedeschia aethiopica* 'Crowborough'

281

282

283

Zebrina

Closely resembling a tradescantia, *Zebrina pendula* is popular because of its strikingly variegated foliage, graceful pendulous habit when mature and adaptability to household conditions. The leaves are green above, striped with silver and purplish-red beneath. The leaves of *Z. purpusii* are a dull purplish-green on the upper side but the lower is a much brighter hue.

Zebrinas can be allowed to grow much bigger than can tradescantias and are perhaps at their best in a hanging basket.

Zephyranthes

One of the less flamboyant of the amaryllis family with flowers, usually short-stemmed, of a simple purity of form that has great beauty. Some species are hardy, like the lovely *Zephyranthes candida* which is also evergreen. Others require only protection from frost and of some the leaves die back in winter. *Z. atamasco* has flowers that are white or tinged with pink; *Z. grandiflora* has flowers of a more uniform pink and *Z. citrina* has deep yellow flowers; there are a number of other attractive species and hybrids.

The smaller species are best packed quite closely in a largish pot but the drainage must be good. The usual principles for watering bulbs apply (q.v.) but they should not be allowed wholly to dry out.

Zygocactus – see CACTI, under *Schlumbèrgera*

Zygopetalum – see ORCHIDS

284. *Zebrina pendula*

285. *Zephyranthes candida*

284

285

Chart of Pests and Diseases

A

B

C

D

E

F

G

H

A. Close-up of green fly aphids

B. Root aphids

C. White fly (*Trialeurodes vaporariorum*)

D. Red spider mite (*Tetranychus urticae*)
Note browning of leaves and abundant webbing.

E. Cyclamen mite (*Steneotarsonemus pallidus*)
Close-up of damaged leaf.

F. Thrips: damage to flower bud

G. Mealy bugs

H. Chrysanthemum leaf miner (*Phytomyza atricornis*)
Close-up of single infested leaf.

I. Root-knot eelworms (*Meloidogyne helpa*)
Transverse section of infected root, showing female containing eggs, and larvae developing in the eggs. All within the root.
(×120 magnification)

J. Caterpillars. Carnation Tortrix (*Cacoecimorpha pronubana*) larva feeding in stem.
(×9 magnification)

K. Scale insects (×3 magnification)

L. Chlorosis (interveinal yellowing of leaf) caused by magnesium deficiency

M. Chrysanthemum rust (*Puccinia chrysanthemi*)
Uredopustule surrounded by characteristic ring of secondary pustules. (×8 magnification)

N. Grey mould fungus (*Botrytis cinerea*) on a plant stem. (×8 magnification)

O. Chrysanthemum mildew

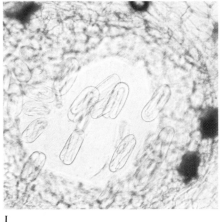

I

J

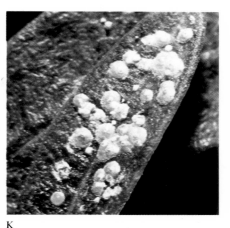

K

L

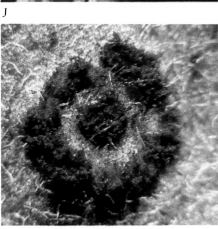

M

N

O

Plants under Families

ACANTHACEAE
Aphelandra
Beloperone
Crossandra
Eranthemum
Fittonia
Hypoestes
Jacobinia
Pachystachys
Pseuderanthemum
Ruellia
Strobilanthes
Thunbergia

AIZOACEAE
Lithops
Mesembryanthemum

AMARYLLIDACEAE
Agave
Amaryllis
Clivia
Eucharis
Galanthus
Haemanthus
Hippeastrum
Hymenocallis
Leucocoryne
Lycoris
Narcissus
Nerine
Sprekelia
Tulbaghia
Vallota
Zephyranthes

APOCYNACEAE
Allamanda
Carissa
Dipladenia
Mandevilla
Nerium
Trachelospermum

ARACEAE
Aglaonema
Anthurium
Arum
Caladium
Dieffenbachia
Monstera
Philodendron
Scindapsus
Spathiphyllum
Zantedeschia

ARALIACEAE
Aralia
Dizygotheca
×Fatshedera
Fatsia
Hedera
Polyscias
Schefflera

ARISTOLOCHIACEAE
Aristolochia

ASCLEPIADACEAE
Ceropegia
Hoya
Stapelia
Stephanotis

BALSAMINACEAE
Impatiens

BEGONIACEAE
Begonia

BIGNONIACEAE
Jacaranda

BORAGINACEAE
Heliotropium

BROMELIACEAE
Aechmea
Billbergia
Cryptanthus
Guzmania
Neoregelia
Nidularium
Tillandsia
Vriesia

CACTACEAE
Chamaecereus
Coryphantha
Echinopsis
Epiphyllum
Espostoa
Lobivia
Mammillaria
Nopalxochia
Notocactus
Rebutia
Rhipsalidopsis
Schlumbergera
Trichocereus

CAMPANULACEAE
Campanula
Trachelium

COMMELINACEAE
Commelina
Cyanotis
Dichorisandra
Rhoeo
Setcreasea
Tradescantia
Zebrina

COMPOSITAE
Chrysanthemum
Euryops
Gerbera
Gynura
Humea
Mutisia
Senecio

CONVOLVULACEAE
Convolvulus
Ipomoea

CRASSULACEAE
Aeonium
Cotyledon
Crassula
Echeveria
Kalanchoe
Rochea
Sedum
Sempervivum

CYPERACEAE
Carex
Cyperus

EPACRIDACEAE
Epacris

ERICACEAE
Erica
Rhododendron

EUPHORBIACEAE
Acalypha
Breynia
Codiaeum
Euphorbia
Jatropha

GENTIANACEAE
Exacum

GERANIACEAE
Pelargonium

GESNERIACEAE
Achimenes
Aeschynanthus
Columnea
Episcia
Gesneria
Hypocyrta
Kohleria
Rechsteineria
Saintpaulia
Sinningia
Smithiantha
Streptocarpus

GRAMINEAE
Bambusa
Oplismenus

IRIDACEAE
Crocus
Freesia
Iris
Ixia
Neomarica

LABIATAE
Coleus
Prostanthera

LAURACEAE
Persea

LEGUMINOSAE
Acacia
Bauhinia
Caesalpinia
Cassia
Chorizema
Clianthus
Cytisus
Erythrina
Lotus
Mimosa

LILIACEAE
Aloe
Asparagus
Aspidistra
Chionodoxa
Chlorophytum
Convallaria
Cordyline
Dracaena
Fritillaria
Gasteria
Gloriosa
Haworthia
Hyacinthus
Lachenalia
Lapageria
Lilium
Muscari
Sansevieria
Scilla
Tulipa
Veltheimia
Yucca

LINACEAE
Reinwardtia

LOGANIACEAE
Desfontainea
Gelsemium

MALPIGHIACEAE
Malpighia

MALVACEAE
Abutilon
Hibiscus

MARANTACEAE
Calathea
Ctenanthe
Maranta
Stromanthe

MELASTOMATACEAE
Centradenia
Medinilla
Sonerila
Tibouchina

MORACEAE
Ficus

MUSACEAE
Musa
Strelitzia

MYRSINACEAE
Ardisia

MYRTACEAE
Callistemon
Eucalyptus
Myrtus

NEPENTHACEAE
Nepenthes

NYCTAGINACEAE
Bougainvillea

OCHNACEAE
Ochna

OLEACEAE
Jasminum
Osmanthus

ONAGRACEAE
Fuchsia

ORCHIDACEAE
Angraecum
Cattleya
Coelogyne
Cymbidium
Dendrobium
Miltonia
Odontoglossum
Paphiopedilum
Sophronitis
Vanda
Zygopetalum

OXALIDACEAE
Oxalis

PALMAE
Butia
Chamaedorea
Chamaerops
Collinia
Dictyosperma
Phoenix
Rhapis
Syagrus
Trithrinax
Washingtonia

PANDANACEAE
Pandanus

PAPAVERACEAE
Dendromecon

PASSIFLORACEAE
Passiflora

PINACEAE
Araucaria

PIPERACEAE
Peperomia
Piper

PITTOSPORACEAE
Pittosporum
Sollya

PLUMBAGINACEAE
Plumbago

POLYGONACEAE
Coccoloba
Muehlenbeckia

POLYPODIACEAE
Adiantum
Asplenium
Blechnum
Cyrtomium
Davallia
Nephrolepsis
Platycerium
Polypodium
Pteris

PRIMULACEAE
Cyclamen
Primula

PROTEACEAE
Grevillea
Stenocarpus

PUNICACEAE
Punica

ROSACEAE
Eriobotrya

RUBIACEAE
Bouvardia
Coffea
Damnacanthus
Gardenia
Hoffmannia
Ixora
Luculia
Manettia
Nertera

RUTACEAE
Boronia
Citrus
Correa
Fortunella

SAPINDACEAE
Litchi

SAXIFRAGACEAE
Bauera
Hydrangea
Saxifraga
Tolmiea

SCHIZAEACEAE
Lygodium

SCROPHULARIACEAE
Allophyton

Calceolaria
Rehmannia

SELAGINELLACEAE
Selaginella

SOLANACEAE
Browallia
Brunfelsia
Capsicum
Cestrum
Datura
Schizanthus
Solanum
Streptosolen

THEACEAE
Camellia

TILIACEAE
Sparmannia

URTICACEAE
Pellionia
Pilea
Soleirolia

VERBENACEAE
Clerodendrum
Duranta
Lantana

VITACEAE
Cissus
Rhoicissus
Tetrastigma

ZINGIBERACEAE
Alpinia
Elettaria
Hedychium
Nicolaia

Index of common names

Adam's Apple – *Citrus aurantifolia*
African Corn Lily – *Ixia*
African Hemp – *Sparmannia africana*
African Violet – *Saintpaulia ionantha*
Alligator Pear – *Persea gratissima*
Aloe, American – *Agave*
Aloe, Partridge-breasted – *Aloe variegata*
Aluminium Plant – *Pilea cadierei*
Amaryllis – see *Hippeastrum*
Amazon Lily – *Eucharis grandiflora*
American Aloe – *Agave*
Angel's Trumpet – *Datura arborea, D. suaveolens*
Arabian Coffee – *Coffea arabica*
Aralia, False – *Dizygotheca elegantissima*
Aralia, Finger – *Dizygotheca elegantissima*
Artillery Plant – *Pilea microphylla*
Arum, Ivy – *Scindapsus*
Arum, Pink – *Zantedeschia rehmannii*
Arum Lily – *Zantedeschia aethiopica*
Asparagus Fern – *Asparagus plumosus*
Aspidistra, Scarlet – *Cordyline*
Atamasco Lily – *Zephyranthes atamasco*
Australian Bluebell Creeper – *Sollya fusiformis*
Australian Fuchsia – *Correa*
Australian Glory Pea – *Clianthus formosus*
Australian Heath – *Epacris longiflora*
Australian Mint – *Prostanthera*
Avocado Pear – *Persea gratissima*
Azalea – see *Rhododendron*

Baby's Tears – *Soleirolia soleirolii*
Balsam, Water – *Impatiens*
Bamboo – *Bambusa*
Banana – *Musa*
Banjo Fig – *Ficus lyrata*
Banyan Tree – *Ficus benghalensis*
Barbados Flower Fence – *Caesalpinia pulcherrima*
Barbados Lily – *Hippeastrum*
Barbados Pride – *Caesalpinia pulcherrima*
Barberton Daisy – *Gerbera*
Bay, Rose – *Nerium oleander*
Bead Plant – *Nertera granadensis*
Belladonna Lily – *Amaryllis belladonna*
Bellflower, Chilean – *Lapageria rosea*
Bellflower, Chimney – *Campanula pyramidalis*
Bellflower, Italian – *Campanula isophylla*
Bermuda Buttercup – *Oxalis cernua*
Bermuda Lily – *Lilium longiflorum*
Bird of Paradise Flower – *Strelitzia*
Bird's Nest Bromeliad – *Nidularium fulgens*
Bird's Nest Fern – *Asplenium nidus*
Bird's Tongue Flower – *Strelitzia*
Black Pepper – *Piper nigrum*

Black-eyed Susan – *Thunbergia alata*
Blood Flower – *Haemanthus*
Blood Lily – *Haemanthus*
Blue Dawn-flower – *Ipomoea learii*
Blue Gum – *Eucalyptus globulus*
Blue Vanda – *Vanda caerulea*
Bluebell Creeper – *Sollya fusiformis*
Boat Lily – *Rhoeo discolor*
Boston Fern – *Nephrolepsis bostoniensis*
Bottle-brush Tree – *Callistemon*
Bow-string Hemp – *Sansevieria*
Brazilian Abutilon – *Abutilon megapotamicum*
Brazilian Edelweiss – *Rechsteineria leucotricha*
Brazilian Mallow – *Abutilon megapotamicum*
Broom, Madeira – *Cytisus × racemosus*
Broom, Teneriffe – *Cytisus supranubius*
Bush Poppy – *Dendromecon rigidum*
Busy Lizzie – *Impatiens*
Buttercup, Bermuda – *Oxalis cernua*
Buttercup Bush – *Cassia*
Butterfly Flower – *Schizanthus*

Cactus, Christmas – *Schlumbergera truncata*
Cactus, Crab – *Schlumbergera truncata*
Cactus, Easter – *Rhipsalidopsis rosea, R. gaertneri*
Cactus, Elephant's Tooth – *Mammillaria*
Cactus, Leaf-flowering – *Epiphyllum ackermannii*
Cactus, Lobster – *Schlumbergera truncata*
Cactus, Mackerel – *Aloe variegata*
Cactus, Nipple – *Mammillaria*
Cactus, Orchid – *Epiphyllum ackermannii*
Cactus, Peanut – *Chamaecereus silvestrii*
Cactus, Pincushion – *Mammillaria bocasana*
Cactus, Powder-puff – *Mammillaria bocasana*
Cactus, Whitsun – *Rhipsalidopsis gaertneri*
Calamondin Orange – *Citrus mitis*
Calico Plant – *Aristolochia elegans*
Californian Bush Poppy – *Dendromecon rigidum*
Calla Lily – *Zantedeschia*
Canary Island Ivy – *Hedera canariensis*
Cane, Dumb – *Dieffenbachia*
Cape Cowslip – *Lachenalia*
Cape Heath – see *Erica*
Cape Jasmine – *Gardenia jasminoides*
Cape Leadwort – *Plumbago auriculata*
Cape Primrose – *Streptocarpus*
Cardamom – *Elettaria cardamomum*
Cardinal's Guard – *Pachystachys coccinea*
Caroline Yellow Jessamine – *Gelsemium sempervirens*
Carrion Flower – *Stapelia*
Cast-iron Plant – *Aspidistra lurida*
Castor-oil Plant, False – *Fatsia japonica*

Cat's Tail, Red-hot – *Acalypha hispida*
Century Plant – *Agave*
Chaplet Flower, Madagascar – *Stephanotis floribunda*
Chenille Plant – *Acalypha hispida*
Cherry Pie – *Heliotropium peruvianum*
Chestnut Vine – *Tetrastigma voinierianum*
Chile Pine – *Araucaria araucana*
Chilean Bellflower – *Lapageria rosea*
Chilean Holly – *Desfontainea*
Chilean Jasmine – *Mandevilla laxa*
Chilli Pepper – *Capsicum annuum*
Chimney Bellflower – *Campanula pyramidalis*
China Orange – *Citrus sinensis*
Chinaman's Pigtail – *Impatiens sultani*
Chinese Evergreen – *Aglaonema*
Chinese Foxglove – *Rehmannia angulata*
Chinese Rose – *Hibiscus rosa-sinensis*
Christmas Bush, Victorian – *Prostanthera lasianthos*
Christmas Cactus – *Schlumbergera truncata*
Christmas Cherry – *Solanum capsicastrum*
Christmas Heather – *Erica gracilis*
Christmas Star Orchid – *Angraecum sesquipedale*
Chusan Palm – *Chamaerops*
Cineraria – *Senecio cruentus*
Climbing Fig – *Ficus pumila*
Climbing Lily – *Gloriosa*
Clog Plant – *Hypocyrta glabra, H. radicans*
Club-moss, Resurrection – *Selaginella lepidophylla*
Clustered Wax Flower – *Stephanotis floribunda*
Coconut Palm – *Syagrus weddeliana*
Coffee – *Coffea arabica*
Cootamunda Wattle – *Acacia baileyana*
Coral Gem – *Lotus bertholetti*
Coral Plant – *Jatropha multifida*
Coral Tree – *Erythrina crista-galli*
Corn Lily, African – *Ixia*
Cowslip, Cape – *Lachenalia*
Crab Cactus – *Schlumbergera truncata*
Crane Flower – *Strelitzia*
Creeping Fig – *Ficus pumila*
Creeping Lily – *Gloriosa*
Creeping Moss – *Selaginella*
Croton – see *Codiaeum variegatum pictum*
Crown of Thorns – *Euphorbia milii*
Cupid's Bower – *Achimenes*

Daffodil – *Narcissus*
Daffodil, Peruvian – *Hymenocallis*
Daisy, Barberton – *Gerbera*
Daisy, Transvaal – *Gerbera*
Date Palm – *Phoenix dactylifera*

Dawn-flower, Blue – *Ipomoea learii*
Day Flower – *Commelina*
Desert Pea, Sturt's – *Clianthus formosus*
Desert Privet – *Peperomia obtusifolia*
Devil's Ivy – *Scindapsus*
Dogwood, Victorian – *Prostanthera lasianthos*
Dr Thomson's Rhododendron – *Rhododendron thomsonii*
Dragon Plant – *Dracaena deremensis*
Dragon Tree, Flaming – *Cordyline*
Duckweed, Fruiting – *Nertera granadensis*
Dumb Cane – *Dieffenbachia*
Dutchman's Pipe – *Aristolochia*
Dwarf Fan Palm – *Chamaerops humilis*
Dwarf Palm – *Collinia elegans*
Dwarf Windmill Palm – *Chamaerops humilis*

Earth Star – *Cryptanthus bivittatus*
Easter Cactus – *Rhipsalidopsis rosea, R. gaertneri*
Easter Lily – *Lilium longiflorum*
Ebony, Mountain – *Bauhinia*
Ebony Tree, Mimosa-leaved – *Jacaranda mimosifolia*
Edelweiss, Brazilian – *Rechsteineria leucotricha*
Elder, Pepper – *Peperomia*
Elephant's Tooth Cactus – *Mammillaria*
Elk's-horn Fern – *Platycerium*

Fairy Primrose – *Primula malacoides*
False Aralia – *Dizygotheca*
False Castor-oil Plant – *Fatsia*
False Jasmine – *Gelsemium sempervirens*
Fan Palm – *Chamaerops humilis*
Fern, Asparagus – *Asparagus plumosus*
Fern, Bird's Nest – *Asplenium nidus*
Fern, Boston – *Nephrolepsis bostoniensis*
Fern, Elk's-horn – *Platycerium*
Fern, Hare's-foot – *Davallia canariensis*
Fern, Holly – *Cyrtomium falcatum*
Fern, Ladder – *Nephrolepsis*
Fern, Maidenhair – *Adiantum*
Fern, Ribbon – *Pteris cretica*
Fern, Shield – *Cyrtomium falcatum*
Fern, Stag's-horn – *Platycerium*
Fern, Sword – *Nephrolepsis*
Fiddle-leaf Fig – *Ficus lyrata*
Fig, Banjo – *Ficus lyrata*
Fig, Climbing – *Ficus pumila*
Fig, Common – *Ficus carica*
Fig, Creeping – *Ficus pumila*
Fig, Fiddle-leaf – *Ficus lyrata*
Fig, Laurel – *Ficus microcarpa*
Fig, Mistletoe – *Ficus deltoidea*
Fig, Weeping – *Ficus benjamina*
Fig-leaf Palm – *Fatsia japonica*
Finger Aralia – *Dizygotheca*
Flame Nettle – *Coleus*
Flame Pea, Holly – *Chorizema ilicifolium*
Flaming Dragon Tree – *Cordyline*
Flamingo Plant – *Anthurium*
Football Plant – *Peperomia argyreia*
Foxglove, Chinese – *Rehmannia angulata*
Foxglove, Mexican – *Allophyton*
Friendship Plant – *Pilea cadierei*
Fritillary, Snake's-head – *Fritillaria meleagris*
Fruiting Duckweed – *Nertera granadensis*
Fuchsia, Australian – *Correa*
Fuchsia, Native – *Correa*
Fuchsia, Water – *Impatiens*

Gem, Coral – *Lotus bertholetti*
Genista – *Cytisus canariensis*
Geranium – *Pelargonium*
Geranium, Horseshoe – *Pelargonium zonale*
Geranium, Ivy-leaved – *Pelargonium peltatum*
Geranium, Nettle – *Coleus*
Geranium, Strawberry – *Saxifraga stolonifera*
Geranium, Zonal – *Pelargonium zonale*
Ginger Lily – *Hedychium gardnerianum*
Glory Bush – *Tibouchina semidecandra*
Glory Lily – *Gloriosa*
Glory, Morning – *Ipomoea tricolor*
Glory of the Snow – *Chionodoxa*
Glory of the Sun – *Leucocoryne ixioides*
Glory Pea – *Clianthus formosus*
Gloxinia – *Sinningia speciosa*
Golden Shower – *Cassia fistula*
Golden Spider Lily – *Lycoris aurea*
Golden-rayed Lily of Japan – *Lilium auratum*
Grape Hyacinth – *Muscari*

Grape Ivy – *Rhoicissus rhomboidea*
Grape, Seaside – *Coccoloba uvifera*
Grapefruit – *Citrus paradisi*
Granadilla – *Passiflora quadrangularis*
Green Wattle – *Acacia decurrens*
Guard, Cardinal's – *Pachystachys coccinea*
Guatemala Rhubarb – *Jatropha podagrica*
Guernsey Lily – *Nerine sarniensis*
Guinea Pepper – *Capsicum annuum*
Gum, Blue – *Eucalyptus globulus*
Gum, Lemon Scented – *Eucalyptus citriodora*
Gum, Round-leaved Snow – *Eucalyptus perriniana*
Gum, Scarlet-flowered – *Eucalyptus ficifolia*
Gum, Simmond's Peppermint – *Eucalyptus simmondsii*
Gunpowder Plant – *Pilea microphylla*

Hairy Wattle – *Acacia pubescens*
Hare's-foot Fern – *Davallia canariensis*
Heath, Australian – *Epacris longiflora*
Heather, Christmas – *Erica gracilis*
Heliotrope, Common – *Heliotropium peruvianum*
Hemp, African – *Sparmannia africana*
Hemp, Bow-string – *Sansevieria*
Holly, Chilean – *Desfontainea*
Holly Fern – *Cyrtomium falcatum*
Holly Flame Pea – *Chorizema ilicifolium*
Horseshoe Geranium – *Pelargonium zonale*
House Lime – *Sparmannia africana*
Houseleek – *Sempervivum*
Humble Plant – *Mimosa pudica*
Husband-and-Wife Plant – *Maranta leuconeura*
Hyacinth, Grape – *Muscari*
Hydrangea, Common – *Hydrangea macrophylla*

Ichang Lemon – *Citrus ichangense*
Incense Plant – *Humea elegans*
Indian Azalea – *Rhododendron simsii*
Indian Laburnum – *Cassia fistula*
Indiarubber Plant – *Ficus elastica*
Iron Cross Begonia – *Begonia masoniana*
Italian Bellflower – *Campanula isophylla*
Ivy Arum – *Scindapsus*
Ivy, Canary Island – *Hedera canariensis*
Ivy, Common – *Hedera helix*
Ivy, Devil's – *Scindapsus*
Ivy, Grape – *Rhoicissus rhomboidea*
Ivy Tree – × *Fatshedera*
Ivy-leaved Geranium – *Pelargonium peltatum*

Jacobean Lily – *Sprekelia formosissima*
Jade Plant – *Crassula portulacea*
Japanese Loquat – *Eriobotrya japonica*
Jasmine, Cape – *Gardenia jasminoides*
Jasmine, Chilean – *Mandevilla laxa*
Jasmine, Common – *Jasminum officinale*
Jasmine, False – *Gelsemium sempervirens*
Jasmine, Madagascar – *Stephanotis floribunda*
Jerusalem Cherry – *Solanum pseudocapsicum*
Jessamine, Caroline Yellow – *Gelsemium sempervirens*
Jessamine, Night-blooming – *Cestrum nocturnum*
Jew, Wandering – *Tradescantia fluminensis* and *Zebrina pendula*

Kaffir Lily – *Clivia miniata*
Kangaroo Thorn – *Acacia armata*
Kangaroo Vine – *Cissus antarctica*
Karo – *Pittosporum crassifolium*
Kumquat – *Fortunella*
Kumquat, Oval – *Fortunella margarita*
Kumquat, Round – *Fortunella japonica*

Laburnum, Indian – *Cassia fistula*
Ladder Fern – *Nephrolepsis*
Lady's Slipper Orchid – *Paphiopedilum*
Laurel Fig – *Ficus microcarpa*
Leadwort, Cape – *Plumbago auriculata*
Leadwort, South African – *Plumbago auriculata*
Leaf-flowering Cactus – *Epiphyllum ackermannii*
Lemon – *Citrus limon*
Lemon, Ichang – *Citrus ichangense*
Lemon Scented Gum – *Eucalyptus citriodora*
Leper's Lily – *Fritillaria meleagris*
Lily, African Corn – *Ixia*
Lily, Amazon – *Eucharis grandiflora*
Lily, Arum – *Zantedeschia aethiopica*
Lily, Atamasco – *Zephyranthes atamasco*
Lily, Barbados – *Hippeastrum*
Lily, Belladonna – *Amaryllis belladonna*

Lily, Bermuda – *Lilium longiflorum*
Lily, Blood – *Haemanthus*
Lily, Boat – *Rhoeo discolor*
Lily, Calla – *Zantedeschia aethiopica*
Lily, Climbing – *Gloriosa*
Lily, Creeping – *Gloriosa*
Lily, Easter – *Lilium longiflorum*
Lily, Ginger – *Hedychium gardnerianum*
Lily, Glory – *Gloriosa*
Lily, Golden Spider – *Lycoris aurea*
Lily, Golden-rayed – *Lilium auratum*
Lily, Guernsey – *Nerine sarniensis*
Lily, Jacobean – *Sprekelia formosissima*
Lily, Kaffir – *Clivia miniata*
Lily, Leper's – *Fritillaria meleagris*
Lily, Madonna – *Lilium candidum*
Lily, Mexican – *Hippeastrum*
Lily of the Nile – *Zantedeschia aethiopica*
Lily of the Palace – *Hippeastrum aulicum*
Lily of the Valley – *Convallaria majalis*
Lily, Peace – *Spathiphyllum*
Lily, Saint Bernard's – *Chlorophytum*
Lily, Scarborough – *Vallota speciosa*
Lily, Spider – *Hymenocallis*
Lily, Trumpet – *Zantedeschia aethiopica*
Lily, White – *Lilium candidum*
Lime, Acid – *Citrus aurantifolia*
Lime, House – *Sparmannia africana*
Lime, Persian – *Citrus limetta*
Lime, Sweet – *Citrus limetta*
Living Stones – *Lithops*
Lizzie, Busy – *Impatiens*
Lobster Cactus – *Schlumbergera truncata*
Lobster-claw – *Erythrina crista-galli*
Loquat – *Eriobotrya japonica*
Lychee – *Litchi*

Mackerel Cactus – *Aloe variegata*
Madagascar Chaplet Flower – *Stephanotis floribunda*
Madagascar Jasmine – *Stephanotis floribunda*
Madeira Broom – *Cytisus × racemosus*
Madonna Lily – *Lilium candidum*
Maidenhair Fern, Common – *Adiantum capillus-veneris*
Mallow, Brazilian – *Abutilon megapotamicum*
Mexican Foxglove – *Allophyton*
Mexican Lily – *Hippeastrum*
Mimosa – *Acacia*
Mimosa-leaved Ebony Tree – *Jacaranda mimosifolia*
'Mind Your Own Business' – *Soleirolia soleirolii*
Ming Tree – *Polyscias*
Mint Bush, Australian – *Prostanthera*
Mistletoe Fig – *Ficus deltoidea*
Monkey Puzzle Tree – *Araucaria araucana*
Morning Glory – *Ipomoea tricolor*
Moss, Creeping – *Selaginella*
Mother-in-law Plant – *Dieffenbachia*
Mother-in-law's Tongue – *Sansevieria*
Mother of Thousands – *Saxifraga stolonifera*
Mountain Ebony – *Bauhinia*
Myrtle, Common – *Myrtus communis*
Myrtle, Tarentum – *Myrtus tarentina*

Natal Plum – *Carissa grandiflora*
Natal Vine – *Rhoicissus rhomboidea*
Native Fuchsia – *Correa*
Nest Fern, Bird's – *Asplenium nidus*
Nettle, Flame – *Coleus*
Nettle Geranium – *Coleus*
Night-blooming Jessamine – *Cestrum nocturnum*
Nile, Lily of – *Zantedeschia aethiopica*
Nipple Cactus – *Mammillaria*
Norfolk Island Pine – *Araucaria excelsa*
Nut, Physic – *Jatropha multifida*

Oak, Silk Bark – *Grevillea robusta*
Oleander, Common – *Nerium oleander*
Orange, Calamondin – *Citrus mitis*
Orange, China – *Citrus sinensis*
Orange, Otaheite Dwarf – *Citrus taitensis*
Orange, Sweet – *Citrus sinensis*
Orchid Cactus – *Epiphyllum ackermannii*
Orchid, Christmas Star – *Angraecum sesquipedale*
Orchid, Lady's Slipper – *Paphiopedilum*
Orchid, Poor Man's – *Schizanthus*
Orchid, Slipper – *Paphiopedilum*
Orchid Tree – *Bauhinia*
Orchid, Venus's Slipper – *Paphiopedilum*
Otaheite Dwarf Orange – *Citrus taitensis*

Oval Kumquat – *Fortunella margarita*

Palace, Lily of the – *Hippeastrum aulicum*
Palm, Chusan – *Chamaerops*
Palm, Coconut – *Syagrus weddeliana*
Palm, Date – *Phoenix dactylifera*
Palm, Dwarf – *Collinia elegans*
Palm, Dwarf Fan – *Chamaerops humilis*
Palm, Fan – *Chamaerops humilis*
Palm, Fig-leaf – *Fatsia japonica*
Palm, Parlour – *Aspidistra lurida*, also
  Chamaedorea elegans bella
Paradise Flower, Bird of – *Strelitzia*
Partridge-breasted Aloe – *Aloe variegata*
Passion Flower – *Passiflora*
Pea, Glory – *Clianthus formosus*
Pea, Holly Flame – *Chorizema ilicifolium*
Pea, Sturt's Desert – *Clianthus formosus*
Peace Lily – *Spathiphyllum*
Peacock Plant – *Calathea mackoyana*
Peanut Cactus – *Chamaecereus silvestrii*
Pear, Alligator – *Persea gratissima*
Pear, Avocado – *Persea gratissima*
Pebble Plants – *Lithops*
Pencil Plant – *Euphorbia tirucalli*
Pepper, Black – *Piper nigrum*
Pepper, Chilli – *Capsicum annuum*
Pepper, Common – *Piper nigrum*
Pepper Elder – *Peperomia*
Pepper, Guinea – *Capsicum annuum*
Pepper, Red – *Capsicum annuum*
Peppermint, Simmond's – *Eucalyptus simmondsii*
Persian Lime – *Citrus limetta*
Peruvian Daffodil – *Hymenocallis*
Physic Nut – *Jatropha multifida*
Pick-a-back Plant – *Tolmiea menziesii*
Pie, Cherry – *Heliotropium peruvianum*
Pigtail, Chinaman's – *Impatiens sultani*
Pincushion Cactus – *Mammillaria bocasana*
Pine, Chile – *Araucaria araucana*
Pine, Norfolk Island – *Araucaria excelsa*
Pine, Screw – *Pandanus*
Pink Arum – *Zantedeschia rehmannii*
Pipe, Dutchman's – *Aristolochia*
Pistol Plant – *Pilea microphylla*
Pitcher Plant – *Nepenthes*
Plum, Natal – *Carissa grandiflora*
Plume, Scarlet – *Euphorbia fulgens*
Poinsettia – *Euphorbia pulcherrima*
Pomegranate – *Punica granatum*
Pomelo – *Citrus paradisi*
Poor Man's Orchid – *Schizanthus*
Poppy, Californian Bush – *Dendromecon rigidum*
Porcelain Flower – *Hoya carnosa*
Powder-puff Cactus – *Mammillaria bocasana*
Prayer Plant – *Maranta*
Pride, Barbados – *Caesalpinia pulcherrima*
Primrose, Cape – *Streptocarpus*
Primrose, Fairy – *Primula malacoides*
Privet, Desert – *Peperomia obtusifolia*
Pudding-pipe Tree – *Cassia fistula*

Queensland Wattle – *Acacia podalyriifolia*

Red Pepper – *Capsicum annuum*
Red-flowered Gum – *Eucalyptus ficifolia*
Red-hot Cat's Tail – *Acalypha hispida*
Regal Pelargonium – *Pelargonium × domesticum*
Resurrection Club-moss – *Selaginella lepidophylla*
Rhododendron, Dr. Thomson's – *Rhododendron
  thomsonii*
Rhubarb, Guatemala – *Jatropha podagrica*
Ribbon Fern – *Pteris cretica*
Rose Bay – *Nerium oleander*
Round Kumquat – *Fortunella japonica*
Round-leaved Snow Gum – *Eucalyptus perriniana*
Roving Sailor – *Saxifraga stolonifera*
Rubber Plant – *Ficus elastica*
Rugby Football Plant – *Peperomia argyreia*

Sailor, Roving – *Saxifraga stolonifera*
Sails, White – *Spathiphyllum wallisii*
Saint Bernard's Lily – *Chlorophytum*
Scarborough Lily – *Vallota speciosa*
Scarlet Aspidistra – *Cordyline*
Scarlet Plume – *Euphorbia fulgens*
Scarlet-flowered Gum – *Eucalyptus ficifolia*
Scented Boronia – *Boronia megastigma*
Screw Pine – *Pandanus*
Seaside Grape – *Coccoloba uvifera*

Sedge – see *Carex*
Sensitive Plant – *Mimosa sensitiva* (also sometimes
  applied to *M. pudica*)
Shield Fern – *Cyrtomium falcatum*
Shingle Plant – *Monstera deliciosa*
Shoe Flower – *Hibiscus rosa-sinensis*
Shower, Golden – *Cassia fistula*
Shrimp Plant – *Beloperone guttata*
Silk Bark Oak – *Grevillea robusta*
Silver Vine – *Scindapsus pictus*
Silver Wattle – *Acacia dealbata*
Simmond's Peppermint – *Eucalyptus simmondsii*
Slipper Flower – *Calceolaria*
Slipper Orchid – *Paphiopedilum*
Snake Plant – *Sansevieria*
Snake's-head Fritillary – *Fritillaria meleagris*
Snow Bush – *Breynia nivosa*
Snow Flower – *Coelogyne cristata*
Snow, Glory of the – *Chionodoxa*
Snow Gum, Round-leaved – *Eucalyptus perriniana*
Snowdrop, Common – *Galanthus nivalis*
South African Leadwort – *Plumbago auriculata*
Spear Flower – *Ardisia crispa*
Spider Lily – *Hymenocallis*
Spider Lily, Golden – *Lycoris aurea*
Spider Plant – *Chlorophytum*, also *Dizygotheca
  elegantissima*
Spleenwort – *Asplenium*
Squill – *Scilla*
Staghorn Fern – *Platycerium*
Star, Christmas – *Angraecum sesquipedale*
Star, Earth – *Cryptanthus bivittatus*
Starfish Flower – *Stapelia*
Starfish Plant – *Cryptanthus bivittatus*
Stompdoorn – *Gardenia thunbergia*
Stonecrop – *Sedum acre*
Stones, Living – *Lithops*
Strawberry Geranium – *Saxifraga stolonifera*
Sturt's Desert Pea – *Clianthus formosus*
Sun, Glory of the – *Leucocoryne ixioides*
Susan, Black-eyed – *Thunbergia alata*
Sweet Lime – *Citrus limetta*
Sweet Orange – *Citrus sinensis*
Sweetheart Vine – *Philodendron scandens*
Swiss Cheese Plant – *Monstera deliciosa*
Sword Fern – *Nephrolepis*

Tail Flower – *Anthurium*
Tarentum Myrtle – *Myrtus tarentina*
Tea Plant – *Camellia sinensis*
Tears, Baby's – *Soleirolia soleirolii*
Teneriffe Broom – *Cytisus supranubius*
Thomson's Rhododendron, Dr – *Rhododendron
  thomsonii*
Thorn, Kangaroo – *Acacia armata*
Thorns, Crown of – *Euphorbia milii*
Thousands, Mother of – *Saxifraga stolonifera*
Throatwort – *Trachelium*
Tiger Plant – *Aphelandra squarrosa*
Toad Flower – *Stapelia*
Tongue Flower, Bird's – *Strelitzia*
Tongue, Mother-in-law's – *Sansevieria*
Tooth Cactus, Elephant's – *Mammillaria*
Transvaal Daisy – *Gerbera*
Trumpet, Angel's – *Datura arborea, D. suaveolens*
Trumpet Lily – *Zantedeschia aethiopica*

Umbrella Plant – *Cyperus alternifolius*
Urn Plant – *Aechmea fasciata*

Vanda, Blue – *Vanda caerulea*
Venus's Slipper – *Paphiopedilum*
Victorian Christmas Bush – *Prostanthera lasianthos*
Victorian Dogwood – *Prostanthera lasianthos*
Vine, Chestnut – *Tetrastigma voinierianum*
Vine, Kangaroo – *Cissus antarctica*
Vine, Natal – *Rhoicissus rhomboidea*
Vine, Silver – *Scindapsus pictus*
Vine, Sweetheart – *Philodendron scandens*
Violet, African – *Saintpaulia ionantha*

Wallpepper – *Sedum acre*
Wandering Jew – *Tradescantia fluminensis* and
  Zebrina pendula
Water Balsam – *Impatiens*
Water Fuchsia – *Impatiens*
Watermelon Peperomia – *Peperomia argyreia*
Wattle, Cootamunda – *Acacia baileyana*
Wattle, Green – *Acacia decurrens*
Wattle, Hairy – *Acacia pubescens*

Wattle, Silver – *Acacia dealbata*
Wattle, Queensland – *Acacia podalyriifolia*
Wax Flower – *Hoya carnosa*
Wax Flower, Clustered – *Stephanotis floribunda*
Weeping Fig – *Ficus benjamina*
White Lily – *Lilium candidum*
White Sails – *Spathiphyllum wallisii*
Whitsun Cactus – *Rhipsalidopsis gaertneri*
Windmill Palm, dwarf – *Chamaerops humilis*
Winter Cherry – *Solanum capsicastrum*

Yellow Jessamine, Caroline – *Gelsemium
  sempervirens*

Zebra Plant – *Aphelandra* and *Calathea zebrina*
Zonal Geranium – *Pelargonium zonale*

Glossary
of botanical terms

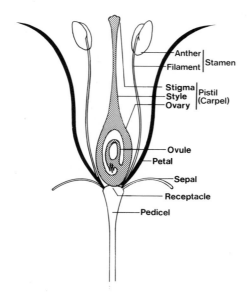

Anther
Filament | Stamen

Stigma
Style | Pistil (Carpel)
Ovary

Ovule
Petal
Sepal
Receptacle
Pedicel

ANTHER
The pollen-bearing end of the stamen (q.v.) of a flower, the male sex cells. The anther may be large as in hibiscus and lilies or small as in primulas.

AXIL
The angle formed by the joint of a leaf or leaf-stalk and a stem of a plant.

BRACT
A modified leaf growing near the calyx (q.v.) on the peduncle or pedicel (q.v.). In some families, such as the Nyctaginaceae to which *Bougainvillea* belongs, the bract is the most showy part of the flower and assumes the place of the petals.

BULB
A much modified shoot or bud, usually formed beneath the ground, with fleshy scales or swollen leaf bases which store food.

CALYX
The outer whorl of floral leaves, usually green, each segment or separate lobe of which is called a sepal (q.v.). When the floral leaves consist of a single whorl, this is often coloured and is usually referred to as the calyx.

CORM
The thickened, solid part of a stem at or just below ground level in which reserve nutritional materials are stored. A bud is produced at the head of a corm and roots from the base. It is distinguished from a bulb (q.v.) by having no separate layers and is very similar to a tuber (q.v.) although corms (e.g. crocus) are surrounded by scales called the 'tunic' whereas tubers are not. They are replaced annually by new corms.

COROLLA
The inner whorl of leaves, the petals, of a flower.

CORONA
An outgrowth of a flower coming between the petals (q.v.) and the stamens (q.v.) as with the crown, cup or trumpet of a narcissus and the 'filaments' or 'rays' of a passion flower.

CORYMB
A more or less flat-topped inflorescence although the flower-stalks spring from different levels; a modified raceme (q.v.).

CULTIVAR
A cultivated variety of a species. The 'cultivar name' is the particular name given to such a variety. *Camellia japonica*, *C. reticulata* and *C. sasanqua* are the species of *Camellia* from which most cultivars have been developed. For example, 'Adolphe Audusson' is a cultivar of *C. japonica*, 'Mary Williams' of *C. reticulata* and 'Narumi-gata' of *C. sasanqua*. 'Cultivar names' are usually descriptive in terms of colour or effect, or names of association, chiefly those of persons. Care is taken to distinguish them from the Latin or Latin-form specific names. Cf variety (q.v.). 'Cultivars' are developed under horticultural conditions whereas 'varieties' develop under natural conditions.

CYME
A branch of flower-heads with the central flower opening first; it may be in the shape of a corymb (q.v.) or of a panicle (q.v.). Cf, in contrast, raceme (q.v.) which is an *unbranched* flower-head.

DISC
(i) A growth from the receptacle of a flower around or at the base of the ovary (see *Kohleria* p. 108);
(ii) the tight-packed centre of the flower of the Compositae (Daisy) family;
(iii) the central part of the lip of an orchid flower.

EPIPHYTE, EPIPHYTIC (adj.)
A plant that grows on another but derives no nourishment specifically from it, in contrast with a parasite which grows on another plant and derives nourishment wholly or partially from it (the host plant). The most important groups of epiphytic plants in this context are the bromeliads and orchids.

FAMILY
After the Order, the family is the broadest classification in the plant kingdom; under each family is grouped the genera, ranging from one genus (q.v.) as in the case of *Rhoeo*, to more than 800 genera in the Compositae, the Daisy family; under each genus are, in turn, grouped the species (q.v.).

Plants of the same family are linked by similarities of flower, fruit and seed (the leaves may be very different in appearance). In some cases, as in the Compositae already cited, the cohesion of family is evident, even superficially. In others like the Euphorbiaceae with the genera *Acalypha*, *Codiaeum*, *Euphorbia*, etc., it is only apparent to a botanist.

FILAMENT
The stalk of a stamen (q.v.), between the anther (q.v.) and the corolla (q.v.).

GENUS
A group of species (q.v.) or in some cases (e.g. *Rhoeo discolor*) one species within a family

GLABROUS   whose flowers, fruit and seed have a similar structure; the leaves may be very different in structure as in the genus *Ficus*. See also 'variety', 'hybrid', 'cultivar'.

GLABROUS   Without hairs. Sometimes used by extension to mean 'smooth'.

GOUTY   Used botanically to describe organic, non-malignant swellings of the stems of certain plants. *Jatropha podagrica* offers an excellent example of this curious development. 'Podagrica' means 'gouty'.

GYNOPHORE   The stalk of an ovary within the calyx (q.v.). The genus *Passiflora*, Passion Flower, which has flowers with conspicuous gynophores derives its name from their supposed resemblance to the instruments of the Crucifixion.

HEEL   Horticulturally one is in many instances advised to take cuttings 'with a heel'. This means that the cutting should consist of a length of new growth together with a length of mature growth which last is called the 'heel'. Some people use 'heel' to refer only to the notch of wood at the end of a stalk when it is pulled away from its joint with the larger stem.

HYBRID   A plant produced by cross fertilizing two species. Such a plant is identified by the sign ×, e.g. *Aeonium × domesticum*. Hybridisation may occur naturally or artificially.

LANCEOLATE   Lance-shaped. Applied to leaves shaped like a lance blade, i.e. considerably longer than they are wide and with pointed tips.

LENTICEL   A pore in the bark of a shrub or tree allowing air to reach the underlying tissue. Lenticels appear as small holes in the surface of the bark containing brownish powder. The lenticels of some of the genus *Polyscias* are particularly pronounced.

NODE   The joint on a stem at which a bud forms, subsequently becoming a leaf or a shoot developing into another stem. The node is usually the point at which growth buds are formed that will develop most readily into roots, hence the importance of the node in a cutting, see p. 12.

PALMATE   Shaped like an open hand. Used to refer to the leaves of plants. The leaves of *Passiflora caerulea* are palmate.

PANICLE   A branched raceme (q.v.) or corymb (q.v.), that is to say a flower-head with separate branches, each ending in a cluster of stalked flowers. The flowers of *Medinilla magnifica* are in the form of a panicle.

PEDICEL, PEDUNCLE   Pedicel means the stalk of a single flower; the final stalk in a panicle (q.v.) between the branch and the flower. Peduncle should be used to describe the *main stalk* of an inflorescence whether in the form of a corymb (q.v.), a raceme (q.v.) or a panicle.

PERIANTH   The outer, non-essential organs of a flower surrounding the sexual organs – usually the sepals and petals. In almost all visually decorative flowers it is the perianth that is the most conspicuous.

PETAL   A division of the corolla (q.v.), usually separate to its base and coloured conspicuously, i.e. not green; petals range from some of the most flamboyant as in *Hibiscus* to the insignificant as in *Polyscias*.

PETIOLE   Leaf stalk.

PINNATE   A pinnate leaf is one in which a series of separate leaflets grow from the leaf stalk as in numerous members of the Leguminosae (the pea family) among them *Acacia*, *Mimosa* etc. or in ferns.

PISTIL   The entire female organ of the flower comprising ovary, style (q.v.) and stigma (q.v.). In many flowers it is roughly the shape of a pestle; hence its name.

RACEME   A branch of flowers from which each flower grows at intervals on an individual stalk.

RHIZOME   A horizontal underground stem, usually creeping, from which shoots and roots sprout. They may be thick and fleshy with stored food.

SCAPE   A leafless flower stem rising directly from the base of the plant. *Hippeastrum* and many other bulbous plants have scapes.

SEPAL   A separate lobe or segment, usually green, of the outer whorl, or calyx (q.v.) of floral leaves. In some flowers the sepals may be brightly coloured and indistinguishable from the petals; also, when there is only a single whorl this is usually referred to in terms of a calyx and is often divided into sepals.

SPADIX   A fleshy flower-head with usually small flowers embedded in its surface. It is often sheathed by a spathe as in many Aroids.

SPATHE   A bract enclosing one or more flowers. It may be unornamental as in a narcissus or else the most conspicuous element in the floral structure as in *Anthurium*.

SPECIES   In terms of plant classification a species is a member of a genus (q.v.); the genus may consist of one or several hundred species whose flowers, fruit or seed have a similar structure.

To justify classification as a separate species a plant must breed true and distinctively in its main characters. See also 'cultivar', 'hybrid' and 'variety'.

STAMEN   The male organ of a flower. The stamen usually consists of a stalk, or filament (q.v.), of varying length, with the pollen-bearing anther (q.v.) at its head which projects from the corolla (q.v.). There may, however, be a 'staminal column' from which the filaments project, as in *Hibiscus*.